Badass Teachers Unite!

Badass Teachers Unite!

Reflections on Education, History, and Youth Activism

Mark Naison

Chicago, Illinois
Haymarket Books

First published by Haymarket Books in 2014
© 2014 Mark Naison

Haymarket Books
PO Box 180165,
Chicago, IL 60618
773-583-7884
info@haymarketbooks.org
www.haymarketbooks.org

ISBN: 978-160846-361-9

Trade distribution:
In the US through Consortium Book Sales
and Distribution, www.cbsd.com
In the UK, Turnaround Publisher Services, www.turnaround-psl.com
All other countries, Publishers Group Worldwide, www.pgw.com

Special discounts are available for bulk purchases by organizations and
institutions. Please contact Haymarket Books for more information at
773-583-7884 or info@haymarketbooks.org.

This book was published with the generous support of Lannan Foundation
and the Wallace Action Fund.

Cover design by Ragina Johnson. Photo of Chicago Teachers Union members
and supporters joining in a mass march after picket duty on the third day of
their September 2012 strike. Photo by Peoples World.

Printed in Canada by union labor.

Library of Congress CIP data is available.

10 9 8 7 6 5 4 3 2 1

Contents

To Liz Phillips—the best educator I know
and maybe the best person

Foreword

Kindergarten through twelfth-grade teachers are under attack. The campaign to convince the public that teachers are the "single most important factor" in school outcomes has become something of a backhanded complement. Teachers are so important that they must be coerced, threatened, punished, micromanaged, demoted, controlled, fired, and in some cases, publicly shamed. Oh yes, teachers are important!

If you're reading these words, there's a good chance that you may have already figured out that the "importance" of teachers correlates with the idea that many other things are less important: class size, resources, child-centered curricula, language, identity, human relationships, compassion, empathy, personal feelings, hunger, racism, and of course, poverty.

If you are a teacher who is reading these words, there's a good chance that the weight of this importance is affecting your health. You are probably experiencing a higher level of stress than normal. You may even have the newly minted "Common Core Syndrome" — symptoms include lack of sleep, loss of appetite, and an urge to update your resume.

If you're sick to death of being maligned, of being micromanaged, over-mandated, overworked, and underappreciated, if you have had enough of being asked to do the impossible, or the ridiculous, or to do things that are bad for children or bad for your colleagues or bad for your community or bad for you (or all of the above), then this book is for you.

If you're a parent or a student reading these words, then chances are you are up to your eyeball in tests and test preparation materials. What's that for homework? Another practice test? Yes, the title of the book indicates that the primary audience is teachers. But anyone who cares about learning, anyone who cares about *real* learning, needs to read this book.

I'm tempted to call it "Chicken Soup for the Teacher's Soul"—but it's more like whiskey. Mark Naison has compiled extremely short pieces of writing about corporate education "reform" and the resistance to it that—not unlike whiskey shots—don't take long to consume but might fuel the fire in your belly.

I first learned Mark Naison's name years ago, before I was a teacher, and before he was writing about teachers. I read it on the cover of a book called *Communists in Harlem during the Depression*. Naison's book stood out because of the way in which he presented a kind of warts-and-all assessment of the work young radicals did in my neck of the woods in tough times. When the landlord literally threw people out of their apartments, they rallied hundreds to put the furniture back in and guard the place. When people couldn't find work, they protested outside Harlem stores to force them to hire local residents. When there weren't enough jobs to go around, they organized sit-ins at the relief centers and got people money to buy food. It's an amazing story, and Naison is a great storyteller.

Years later, when I became a teacher, I worked in Harlem's elementary schools for eight years. I was there when Harlem became Ground Zero for corporate education reform. I was there when Wall Street money came in like a hurricane shattering public schools and inserting charter schools left and right. I watched parents divide over the issue, I participated in countless public hearings and debates, and tried to defend the schools in which I worked from budget cuts and colocations. Naison's stories from the Depression stayed with me and inspired me to try to rally people to defend a local community center from being closed or to stand with parents and teachers against school closures. We rallied, protested, marched, argued, and sang over countless issues large and small. We lost many of those struggles, but my hope is that, in the course of fighting, we helped to create a real debate about corporate education reform, and to puncture the idea that everyone just loves charter schools and standardized tests and can't get enough of them. One hopeful sign was that many of the parents who started out on the charter school side came to our side over time. There were those who said we should be quiet because Harlem parents "love" charter schools. Well, it turns out that that wasn't true for every parent. And many parents, after some experience in those schools, came to realize that they weren't actually the solution they had been promised. Some of those parents started to join us at protests, press conferences, and rallies. Some of these people and their struggles are documented in the film I co-narrated, *The Inconvenient Truth Behind Waiting for Superman*.

Imagine my surprise when, in the midst of all these struggles, Mark Naison's name began to pop up again and again on my computer screen as the author of writings about—of all things—the corporate attack on public education! He was relentlessly posting short articles about the logic of privatization, the movement to defend public education, the importance of teacher-parent-student solidarity, and I was relentlessly devouring them. When I began my doctoral studies in urban education at the CUNY Graduate Center, I immediately sought out Mark for advice about my research ideas. I met him one day in his office at Fordham University. I had no idea what to expect. As it turned out, Mark is one of the most friendly and generous people you might ever meet. What his office lacks in polish (there are piles and piles of books and papers occupying nearly every surface) it makes up in personality and charm—not unlike the man himself. Mark was exceedingly helpful, and I look forward to thanking him in future publications. Hey, I might as well start now. Thanks, Mark!

Many moons later my computer lit up again with news of a new online group: The Badass Teachers Association. I smiled at the idea, but didn't think much of it, until I learned that it claimed (almost overnight) tens of thousands of members. And again, to my surprise, Mark Naison was at the center of it.

But it's not surprising. Mark has been at the center of the struggle for public education nearly his whole life. As you will learn in this book, although he is not a K–12 educator, and not a professor of education, he has remained, as a scholar, intimately connected to New York City's public schools by a thousand strands of intellectual collaboration, research projects, volunteer work, activism, friendship, and family. Mark's heart and soul are in this struggle, and, as you will see, he has put both into this book.

The fight to defend and improve our pubic schools is difficult, exhausting, stressful, challenging, all-consuming and . . . it is one of the most important things we can do in our lives. When you are at the end of your rope, in need of a reminder of what this struggle is all about, of what public schools can and should mean to our communities, to our young people, and to ourselves, I hope you pick up this book and let Mark Naison speak to you. If you've read this far, you're on your way. Enough is enough. It's time we stood up for our schools and our communities. Read on.

Brian Jones
New York City
January 2014

Introduction

During the last ten years, many people have stepped forward to denounce the bipartisan crusade to privatize public education and force it to operate according to business principles. Most have been teachers, school administrators, and education scholars—people whose lives have been spent in the nation's public schools, and whose life's work has been put in jeopardy by the new policies. I came to education activism by a different path.

I am a scholar in African American and labor history, and a longtime coach and community organizer, who found himself working regularly in public schools as a result of a community history initiative I started called the Bronx African American History Project. Starting in 2004, when a social studies coordinator named Phil Panaritis discovered my research and decided to promote it to Bronx teachers and principals, I found myself giving lectures, workshops, and tours to teachers, students, and administrators in more than thirty Bronx schools, and eventually hired to lead two-month community history projects in thirteen elementary schools, middle schools, and high schools. Never, in forty-plus years of teaching and scholarship, did I see research I had done be transformed so creatively, largely by the teachers to whom I made presentations. They leaped upon the chance to get their students to see themselves, and their families, as historical subjects and create films, plays, and exhibits that brought their neighborhoods to life.

Then, with startling suddenness, the projects I was involved in were pushed out of the local schools, and the wonderful teachers I had worked with made targets of a campaign of demonization by elected officials and the media. The main culprit here was the Bloomberg administration, which began a program of school grading and school closures based on student test scores that put every Bronx school on notice that it had best emphasize test prep to the exclusion of anything else. But this approach was also pushed hard by the newly elected Obama administration as part of its "Race to the Top" initiative, and had virtually unanimous support from the press. Not only was the most successful education initiative I had ever worked on being shut down but teachers and principals whom I had most come to admire were being browbeaten, intimidated, micromanaged, and threatened with loss of employment if they didn't do something dramatic to raise test scores. Worse yet, these incredibly hard-working, courageous people—many of whom grew up in the same neighborhoods they taught in—were being blamed for the alleged failures of public schools and the failure of the nation to reduce poverty and inequality.

Although I had never before written about education policy, and had no background as an education researcher, I could not remain silent in the face of what I perceived as a catastrophe for Bronx schools and neighborhoods, especially since the teachers and principals under attack could not speak out on their own behalf without risking their jobs. So I wrote an essay titled "In Defense of Public School Teachers" based on my experience in Bronx schools, posted it on my blog, and sent it around to a small number of activists and scholars I regularly corresponded with [editor's note: the essay is reprinted in this book in part one]. Very quickly, the piece went viral. I began receiving one heartbreaking message after another from public school teachers—in New York and from around the nation—who felt that the whole nation had ganged up on them, and their ability to teach their students was being systematically undermined by policy makers who thought schools should be run like businesses. In their minds, "bad teachers" were causing the United States to fall behind other nations in educational performance.

The more I communicated with teachers—especially those located in schools in high-poverty communities—and with my wife, a principal in a high-performing school in Brooklyn in no danger of being closed but was still deluged with burdensome tests and assessments, the more I became convinced that a policy catastrophe of unprecedented proportions was unfolding in education. As a historian of social movements, and as a participant in some of the great justice movements of the last half of the twentieth century, I felt I had a responsibility to challenge these new policies, put them in historical context, and strip away policymakers' claims to be motivated by concerns for reducing racial and economic inequality. And here, I came upon an incredible and infuriating irony. The more I looked into the new policies—judging schools and teachers on the basis of test scores; closing allegedly "failing" schools; taking power away from elected school boards and teachers unions; giving extreme preference to charter schools—the more I saw that they were designed to benefit powerful business leaders whose wealth had grown incrementally in the last thirty years. Despite egalitarian pretensions, school reform was a preeminently elite strategy designed to weaken the public sector, and open it up to private control and private investment.

There were others who were saying this, but I had firsthand knowledge through my research and my own experiences of schools in the Bronx over the last seventy years. I knew what kinds of programs and pedagogies had engaged and failed to engage working-class students and children of color who had attended those schools. More than one hundred of the three hundred–plus oral history interviews we conducted for the Bronx African American History Project dealt with school experiences, in some cases going back to the late 1930s and early 1940s, and these accounts provided a rich resource and enabled us to put current reform efforts in historical context. There were more than a few success stories in these narratives. What had worked to motivate and engage Bronx students of color, past and present, often derived from elements deemphasized by the current generation of school "reformers"—arts, music, sports, after-school programs, and teacher mentoring. Schools in the Bronx, when they worked the best, were round-the-clock community centers open from dawn to dusk, with teachers or coaches whose personal intervention often had greater, lasting,

positive effects on students than classroom instruction designed to prepare
for a test. Everything I had learned from my interview subjects, several of
whom went on to be teachers, principals, and school superintendents, challenged the idea that punishing and rewarding teachers on the basis of student
test scores would be the best way to improve schools in low- and moder-
ate-income neighborhoods. So I began to write about what kind of programs
could improve schools in communities of color, and critique those that I
thought would make them worse. I was horrified to discover that virtually
nothing I suggested had the slightest bit of currency with those making education policy at the local, state, or national level.

Since speaking truth to power was clearly failing, I started turning my
attention to the question of how people so resistant to the voices of lifetime
educators had managed to engineer a virtual coup d'état in the sphere of
education policy, and pursuade politicians in both parties to give them unlimited power to reshape the nation's schools. Here my historical studies
proved to be of some value. I recognized that two previous examples of bipartisan initiatives based on false assumptions had put the nation through
more than a decade of hell—Prohibition and the war in Vietnam—and used
those analogies to let people know that, yes, current school reform policies
are much more likely to undermine the nation's schools and maximize existing inequalities than to remedy them. Indeed, that policies this destructive
have held sway in our nation before. I also made the argument that the only
way policies so destructive, and so immune to common sense, came to dom-
inate is that the extreme concentration of wealth at the very top layers of
society has given a small number of wealthy individuals—in this case Bill
Gates, Michael Bloomberg, Eli Broad, the Waltons, the Koch brothers, and
a coterie of hedge fund leaders—the power to totally control policy discourse in the media and the political arena, making a mockery of democratic
ideals and practice. How else could you have a discourse about "improving
teaching" that drives teacher morale to its lowest levels in recorded history;
that advertises its civil rights aspirations but denies people in poor communities any input into policy decisions; and extols testing and standardized
curricula in public schools while leaving private schools (where most policy
makers send their own children) totally untouched by such "reforms"? In
essence, I was arguing that those shaping education policy were guilty of

crimes of historic proportions against American children and of undermining a noble profession for selfish interests and, in some instances, profits.

As my argument focused increasingly on the profound illegitimacy of policies wrapped in the mantles of patriotism, philanthropy, and civil rights, I found myself also addressing the question of organizing—how do we resist policies that appear to command such overwhelming power? Here I turned to other examples in US history where people deemed weak and unorganizable by those who ruled them changed the course of history with bold actions, whether it was autoworkers seizing factories in Flint, Michigan; college students seizing buildings at Columbia University with high school students mobilizing their support; or Dr. King mobilizing high school and junior high school students to march into downtown Birmingham in the face of police dogs and fire hoses. I also drew upon the examples of Occupy Wall Street, the Greensboro student sit-ins, and draft resistance during the war in Vietnam to show how resistance movements can seemingly spring out of nowhere and take surprising forms. I suggested this would unfold in the resistance of parents, teachers, and students to corporate education reform. My message, which I repeated in essay after essay and speech after speech, was that no ruling class, or dominant elite, can permanently immunize itself to the forces of resistance. No group is so beaten down and oppressed that it cannot find weaknesses in the armor of the ruling elites.

To summarize, if my voice is unusual among the many speaking up to challenge attacks on teachers and public schools, it stems from my commitment to try to understand current policy initiatives in light of the historic experience of immigrants and people of color in Bronx schools and the history of great human rights struggles in US history. These perspectives infuse me with what some might regard as unjustified optimism. But having spent my life studying how people written off by those in power and their own leaders as inert, passive, and apathetic, have leaped into action and forced their voices to be heard and changed policies for the better, I am convinced that corporate school reform, albeit after doing immense damage, is generating a powerful enough opposition to force in a new direction the nation's education discourse and policy.

And wouldn't you know it, in the last three months, a new group has arisen—with a most improbable name—the Badass Teachers Association.

The Badass Teachers Association has taken resistance to corporate school reform to new levels, with its thirty-six thousand members (and growing) coordinating national actions against reform figures ranging from Bill Gates, Arne Duncan, and Michelle Rhee to Rahm Emanuel, the Waltons, and the American Legislative Exchange Council (ALEC). And its growth comes on the heels of a test revolt in New York State that was built on an equally improbable alliance of libertarians, conservatives, liberals, and leftists.

History is full of surprises, and I hope you can find examples that will encourage you to make some history of your own in the pages that follow! As this book's title suggests, Badass Teachers Unite!

Brooklyn, New York
January 2014

Part 1:

**Education Policy Critique
and Advocacy**

My Thoughts on "Educational Reform"

Speaking on behalf of "students," especially students of color, an entire generation of self-described educational reformers have systematically undermined the teaching profession making graduation rates and performance on standardized tests the primary measures of value in classrooms. Has this educational revolution, now in progress for almost fifteen years, contributed to greater economic and social equality in the United States?

The statistics show otherwise. The wealth gap in the nation and in New York City has continued to widen despite the imposition of a test-centered approach to public education. Trying to achieve social equality through public education when tax, health care, and investment policies move in opposite directions, is proving to be a fool's errand.

Not only isn't it working economically, it is putting students from poor and working-class families at a disadvantage by forcing creativity and critical thinking skills out of the classroom in favor of skills easily measured on standardized tests. From an administrative standpoint, it all makes sense—let's look for results that can be easily measured. From the teachers' standpoint, it looks like a conspiracy to remove creativity and agency from their practice, while creating a new class of administrators who view teachers as pieces on a chessboard.

In Defense
of Public School Teachers

There are few jobs in this country more challenging than that of a public school teacher. In a country with one of the highest rates of poverty in the industrialized world and almost no social safety net to help struggling families, our teachers have to create a positive learning atmospheres in classrooms filled with young people under stress. The teacher not only has to be someone who can transmit knowledge and skills, he or she has to be a diplomat, a counselor, a surrogate parent, and occasionally a police officer. And those skills don't just extend to the students. The parents and caretakers (because many working-class and poor children live with grandparents or foster parents) can also be challenging because many of them are under extreme stress, and can "act out" almost as much as their children. Local school boards and state authorities, that are putting teachers under pressure to have their students pass standardized tests and are looking to discipline and fire teachers if they do not produced the desired results, are also a problem. A teacher today faces a complex variety of tasks that few people confront on their jobs—tasks that require intellect, creativity, patience, imagination, and if all those fail, sheer stubbornness and courage.

Given the difficulty of the tasks that teachers confront, the incredibly long hours they spend preparing lessons and grading assignments, as well as the tremendous time and expense they put into outfitting their classrooms, you would think that teachers would be revered and respected by the American public. But, in fact, the contrary is true. Americans, more than any people on the globe, seem to resent and even hate teachers!

How else to explain the propensity of people on all sides of the political spectrum to blame teachers for the persistence of poverty in the United States, for the failure of the United States to be economically competitive with other nations, and for disappointing test scores and graduation rates among racial minorities? We have the spectacles of the president of the United States praising the mass firing of teachers in a working-class town in Rhode

Island where test scores were low. The school chancellor in the nation's largest city demanded the publication of confidential—and often misleading—teacher rating data in the press and a mass-market film about the power of teachers focused exclusively on privately funded charter schools, conveniently leaving out the thousands of dedicated; and often brilliant public school teachers working in the nation's high-poverty districts.

As the child of two New York City public school teachers who each spent more than thirty years in the system, and as someone who spends a good deal of time interacting with teachers in Bronx schools, I find this hostility to teachers totally misguided. I invite anyone who thinks teachers are to blame for poverty and inequality to come with me on my trips to Bronx public schools and see the extraordinary efforts that teachers and principals make to create learning environments that are filled with excitement, stimulation, and even beauty. Look at the ways classrooms and hallways are decorated. See the incredible projects teachers do with their students. See the plays and musical performances that the schools put on. And talk to the teachers and principals about what their students are up against. I will never forget the closed-door meeting I had with a Bronx principal whose school served three meals a day. He described how many of his children started crying on Friday because they were afraid they wouldn't eat until they came back to school on Monday. Or speak with a teacher who is working in a class where half the students don't live with their biological parents, and you'll get a sense of the desperate needs these children have for love and affection.

I would like to know how well Secretary of Education Arne Duncan or New York City schools chancellor Joel Klein would do prepping students for tests if they taught in a Bronx middle school or high school where half the students are on the verge of dropping out because of family pressures, or problems reading and writing in English. The teachers who come to these schools and give students love, as well as instruction, are not cynically collecting paychecks. They are taking responsibility for problems our society neglects and for family and community services we fail to provide.

We live in a society without adequate daycare, health care, and recreation for working-class families, where people have to work two or three jobs to stay in their apartments or share those apartments with multiple strangers. Today young people face violence and stress in their living quarters, as well as on the streets, and sports programs and music programs are only available for those who can pay. It's not surprising that public schoolteachers have one of the hardest jobs in society.

They deserve respect and support, not contempt. They are among America's true heroes.

TUESDAY, DECEMBER 28, 2010

A Teacher's Lament: What I Do Best Matters Least

If anyone ever asked me what I would most like to be remembered for, I would answer without hesitation "my teaching." Teaching wakes me up in the morning and keeps me up at night. I think about how to motivate my students when I am reading, listening to music, or talking to my friends, and stay in touch with my students long after they have graduated. When I give a lecture where everything comes together exactly as I planned, and my students clearly "get" what I am trying to say, I feel like Bruce Springsteen, Janis Joplin, or Jimi Hendrix after a performance—exhausted and emotionally drained but ready to recharge my batteries and do it again! I have found nothing that compares to the high of helping my students see the world in new ways, and helping them find powers inside themselves that they didn't know were there.

But while the thrill of teaching motivated me to get a PhD in the first place, it had virtually nothing to do with my professional advancement. Every time I have received a promotion, it has been on the strength of my published writings or the research I have done. I benefit from tremendous support of the Fordham University administration, and I am treated with considerable respect by my professional colleagues, but I doubt if much of it derives from what goes on in my classroom. The only people who know, or care, about the time and effort I put into my teaching are my students. It is their responses and their accomplishments that affirms my value as a teacher.

I am not complaining about my personal situation, which is, at the very least, a privileged one. But I do want to point out how little teaching is valued and understood, in American society. Because so many of the qualities that make a great teacher—particularly the ability to forge emotional connections with students—cannot be easily quantified, it is tempting to see teaching as something that anyone can do: view teachers as replaceable parts, see teaching as a "necessary evil" for scholars whose "real work" is research.

This attitude toward teaching is damaging at all levels, but particularly in elementary and secondary education. The best people enter teaching because they want to change lives, but when policy makers devalue the emotional connections teachers make with students in favor of "success" on standardized tests, this pushes great teachers out of the profession.

When teaching is reduced to its capacity to generate short-term performance under conditions of extreme stress, you not only take most of the joy out of teaching and learning is removed, and the capacity of teachers to stir the imaginations of their students and inspire them to do great things is undermined. Mastery of a defined body of knowledge is only one portion of a teacher's job; teachers also want to make learning joyful and exciting. If you base evaluation of teaching only on the first element, because it is the only thing that can be measured, teachers are penalized for employing creativity and can also make students hate school. This is precisely what the education reform movement institutionalized by No Child Left Behind and Race to the Top has done. It has created a legion of browbeaten and demoralized teachers, and fostered a lifetime aversion to education among young people in working-class and poor communities. They have been drilled and drilled, tested and tested, and their remarkable creative talents are going unrecognized and untapped.

If education is going to thrive in America, including in the poorest and most socially isolated communities, we need to recruit and retain teachers who love teaching, and treat them with respect. Salary is one component of this, but autonomy is another. If teachers don't have the freedom to be creative and create emotional connections with students and their families, then you will simply reproduce the existing structure of race and class inequality in the next generation. We need to view students as creative thinkers and makers of their own destinies, not as obedient and subservient drones who recapitulate bodies of knowledge in easily digestible forms. And this requires having teachers who can strike balances between skills instruction and tapping students' imaginative and creative sides. Many of those teachers are already there, ready to be unleashed; others are waiting to be recruited to the profession.

But until education reform becomes "teacher centered," instead of being infused with managerial imperatives and obsessed with accountability, our education system, at all levels, will remain stagnant.

There are great teachers everywhere. If we honor them and reward them, maybe we can bring back joy and creativity to our schools.

TUESDAY, NOVEMBER 23, 2010
Erasing History: A Key Feature of the Bloomberg/Klein Regime in the New York City Public Schools

One of the characteristics of all dictatorial regimes is the rewriting of history to enhance the regime's claim to leadership. This was done by European colonialists; Soviet Communists; third world dictators like Rafael Trujillo and Idi Amin,; and, for a very long time, by white supremacists in the United States who systematically erased all achievements by African Americans from the historical record.

The Bloomberg-Klein team in charge of the New York City school system has made it seem that New York City public schools were scandalously flawed and injurious to New York City schoolchildren before they took over. Furthermore, racially charged rhetoric has been a major weapon in the campaign of intimidation the Klein Department of Education which imposed a rigid test driven regime upon teachers and principals. In a conversation with me, one CUNY administrator allied with them called the New York City schools pre-Klein/Bloomberg a "criminal conspiracy against black and Latino children."

If you have not spent much time in New York City's public schools, or have had little personal contact with longtime teachers and administrators, you might find this analysis believable. But as someone brought up by two parents who were lifelong teachers (at Jamaica HS and Eli Whitney Vocational HS), who were revered by their students and colleagues, and who is married to a principal who is a legend in her school and neighborhood, I was predisposed to be skeptical of the Bloomberg-Klein portrait of what went on in New York City schools prior to their arrival.

But my experience I have had bringing the research of the Bronx African American History Project into Bronx schools has really brought home the absurdity and injustice of their campaign. Over the past seven years, I have spent time in more than thirty Bronx elementary schools, middle schools, and high schools, giving lectures and tours, doing teacher training, speaking at graduation ceremonies, and sponsoring schoolwide oral history festivals. And my experience with teachers in those schools totally contradicted the image of a pre-Klein educational wasteland that the DOE has promulgated.

First of all, the vast majority of teachers and principals who brought me into the schools to help incorporate community history into their classrooms are veterans of the New York City public school system. They include Phil Panaritis, the head of social studies at a Bronx district who first brought me in to present our research to teachers in his district; Julia Swann, the network leader who had me do oral history training in the thirteen schools in her charge; Gary Israel, the brilliant teacher and robotics coach who brought me in to help create a museum in Morris High School; and Paul Cannon, the visionary principal who had our research team help him organize his entire school culture around community history. The most impressive people I have encountered in Bronx schools have been longtime veterans of the New York City public school system, not hotshot young teachers brought in by alternative certification programs.

Each of these individuals are passionately committed to educational equity, and they working to inspire and empower students long before the Bloomberg-Klein team took charge of the schools. Many were products of the New York City public schools themselves.

And they are not alone. During the course of the lectures, workshops, and tours that I give in Bronx schools (I average two per month), I have met hundreds of veteran teachers who are intellectually curious, invested in their students' well-being, and determined to try anything that will instill a love of learning in the children they work with. These people were all in the New York City school system long before Michael Bloomberg became mayor.

Devaluing their accomplishments and erasing them from history does violence to the real history of the New York City school system and gives DOE leaders license to implement policies that take power away from teachers by imposing a regime of rote learning and test preparation that is more likely to harm than help students.

SUNDAY, SEPTEMBER 26, 2010

"Educational Reformers" Neglect Need for Vocational and Technical Education

At a time when there is a huge need for technical/vocational education, vocational high schools are being shut down, and are being replaced by small high schools or charter schools that, when they work at all, train students for white-collar occupations. To rebuild our infrastructure and shift to a green economy, we need engineers, electricians, and construction workers, not just clerks and brokers! But those with a "one size fits all" approach to educational reform fail to see this.

The irrationality of this hit home several months ago when I learned that Alfred E. Smith Vocational and Technical High School in the South Bronx was designated as one of twenty schools to be closed by the New York City Department of Education because of low test scores. I had visited Alfred E. Smith last November to do a book event for Allen Jones's Bronx memoir *The Rat That Got Away* and was tremendously impressed by the high morale of students and teachers, as well as the huge auto repair shops in the school. I remember thinking how valuable an institution this was in the Bronx, where auto repair shops and body shops are among the most thriving of local businesses. When I discovered the school was slated for closure, I was astonished. In a community where unemployment rates for black and Latino youth approach 50 percent, DOE leaders have chosen to close one school that actually trains them for decent-paying jobs in their own community!

But the educational reformers, who seem to have "drunk their own Kool-Aid," never let history, local conditions, or common sense curb the mechanical application of their test-driven models. Other advanced nations, like Germany, have actually invested *more* in technical education to help their citizens acquire the mechanical skills to adapt to a green economy. there will be millions of unfilled skilled mechanical jobs when (if?) the United States makes such a transition.

Someday, and I hope it is soon, people will challenge the union-busting, test-obsessed, charter-school-promoting lawyers and executives trying to remake American education and develop a teacher-centered, student-centered, community-centered approach that recognizes the wide variety of skills needed to have a viable economy.

Fortunately, this is happening in New York. Thanks to a lawsuit supported by the NAACP and others, the closure of Alfred E. Smith High School has been halted.

SUNDAY, NOVEMBER 6, 2011
Why Teachers Must Become Community Organizers and Justice Fighters

There is a long history of teacher activism in the United States. In New York City, the tradition goes back to the late 1930s when teachers associated with the Communist Party and the New York City Teachers Union fought to have Negro History Month honored in the New York City public schools; force the replacement or reassignment of racist teachers; and challenge the placement of black students in the lowest tracks and most decayed schools. This legacy of antiracist activism, always done in collaboration with civil rights organizations and community groups, lasted into the late '50s when many of the most effective teacher-activists were pushed out of the New York school system during the Cold War. This forgotten tradition is described in depth in Clarence Taylor's book *Reds at the Blackboard: Communism, Civil Rights and the New York City Teachers Union.*

After the old Teachers Union faded from the scene, another group of teacher-activists, drawing upon a broad coalition of liberals, socialists, and moderate trade unionists, won recognition for the United Federation of Teachers (UFT) as official bargaining agent for New York City School teachers, winning them decent salaries, job security, and some level of freedom of expression inside and outside their schools. The UFT, from its outset, worked to improve conditions in schools for all students and supported the nonviolent civil rights struggle in the South and the North. Unfortunately in 1968 the UFT found itself engaged in conflicts with some community leaders in Harlem and Ocean Hill–Brownsville during a series of brutal strikes that challenged community control of school policies in those neighborhoods. These strikes not only created a fissure between UFT and civil rights organizations, it created fissures within the UFT between the strikes' supporters and opponents that left a legacy of bitterness that lasted for years to come.

In the wake of those strikes, the UFT proved powerless to resist a devastating attack on the New York City public schools orchestrated by bankers who dominated the Emergency Financial Control Board (EFCB); the EFCB took the city into financial receivership following the fiscal crisis of 1975. The Board of Education was forced by this unelected body to make budget cuts, and close down world-class music programs in the city's junior high schools; prior to the crisis, most junior high schools had upwards of two hundred musical instruments that were lent out free of charge to anyone who was accepted in their bands or orchestras. The after-school programs and night centers that were a fixture of every public school in the city in the 1940s, 1950s, and 1960s were also eliminated. These programs were never fully replaced, and from the late 1970s on, children had less access to arts, sports, and after-school mentoring than their parents' enjoyed in those very same schools.

Nearly forty years have passed since these fiscal crisis budget cuts, and our public schools now face a challenge more insidious and, perhaps, more formidable. All across the nation, a poisonous coalition of multibillionaire business leaders, test and technology companies, charitable foundations, and elected officials are pushing a nationwide education agenda that involves the introduction of high-stakes testing at all grade levels; evaluation of teachers and schools based on student test scores; and the introduction of "competition" into public education by independently managed charter schools allowed special advantages in funding and recruitment.

This education reform agenda embraced by both the Bush and Obama administrations and embodied in No Child Left Behind and Race to the Top represents a formidable assault on teachers' hard-won collective bargaining rights, as well as their classroom autonomy and freedom of expression. It also represents a devastating attack on children in America's working-class and poor communities at a time when our nation is experiencing an upward redistribution of wealth and a sharp increase in poverty levels. Corporate education reform reduces schooling in the nation's poor communities to test prep and obedience training, squeezing out critical thinking and the arts. It also divides and pits communities against each other by transforming charter schools into privileged enclaves that promise passage out of the neighborhood to a few lucky children, and the remaining public schools, and their students, are viewed aversion and contempt.

Given the complex challenge corporate education reform poses, today's teacher-activists cannot just have a strategy that is solely school or teacher-centered. They must become community organizers who fight school closings, the proliferation of high-stakes tests, and the weakening of teachers' bargaining rights as attacks on the ability of working-class people and people of color to fight for better opportunities for themselves and their children. In this setting, teacher-activists must put forth a vision of radical democracy that envisions education as empowering students to critically think and become agents of historical change, not function as obedient test-takers. This vision situates schools as central to keeping neighborhoods united and mobilized to get a fair share of the nation's resources.

Occupy Wall Street has provided a language and an example to put that model of radical democracy into practice. But it cannot work unless teachers link their fates to those of the students they work with and the people in the communities where their schools are located. Unless teacher-activists become community organizers and justice fighters in the broadest sense, they will not be able to defend their classrooms from the incursions of corporate interests.

A Buffalo Story: How School Turnaround Mandates Undermine Effective Community Organizing

During mid-October, I had the privilege of spending two days getting an in-depth exposure to one of the most radical experiments in democratic urban transformation in the nation—a Choice Neighborhoods initiative on the East Side of Buffalo created by SUNY Buffalo's Center for Urban Studies, in partnership with Buffalo's Municipal Housing Authority and Erie County's community action agency. The brainchild of the Center for Urban Studies visionary leader Dr. Henry Taylor, the initiative seeks to engage residents in some of Buffalo's poorest neighborhood in redesigning and transforming public housing projects, business districts, schools, and vacant properties in the target area. Improving schools is one of the key objectives of the initiative; but it seeks to do that not by insulating schoolchildren from the forces surrounding them and educating them to escape the neighborhood but by engaging them in a democratic, community-planning process along with their teachers, their parents, and neighbors, and by making a problem-centered pedagogy part of the school curriculum. Even before the Choice Grant, the center had gotten students in one of the schools—Futures Academy—in the initiative involved in transforming a rubble-strewn lot across the street from the school into a beautiful park and vegetable garden and another smaller lot nearby into a bird park. The students had also done remarkable arts work for the initiative, both in public spaces and the school. They had become agents of neighborhood change.

What the students had accomplished was nothing short of miraculous, but unfortunately, such accomplishments did not register on the metrics mandated for low-performing schools by No Child Left Behind and Race to the Top, and mechanically applied by the State Education Department in Albany. As a result, Futures Academy—whose school population was drawn from students who could not get into or were pushed out of charter schools and magnet schools—went through three different principals in the ten years the center had worked in it. Each one was forced out solely because of poor student performance on standardized tests. Student participation on democratic neighborhood transformation could not save these principals; they were judged solely on test performance, and Futures Academy, for school administrators, became a revolving door.

While Professor Taylor and his colleagues realize they cannot change educational policies being shaped in Washington and Albany, it is sad to see how these policies place handicaps on what they are trying to accomplish. In a neighborhood where over 90 percent of the residents are black, most are poor, half of the land sits vacant, public transportation is inadequate, and abandoned stores and factories dot local business districts, the public schools are one of the few remaining anchors. They are not only the largest remaining buildings in the East Side neighborhood, they contain space and resources—auditoriums, gymnasiums, classrooms, computer labs—which could be vital assets to all residents as they participate in this project. Professor Taylor's goal, through in-school and after-school programs, is to enlist public school students in every part of the neighborhood redevelopment initiative, including public art projects, neighborhood beautification initiatives, urban agriculture, redesigning local business districts, and imagining new neighborhood institutions that enhance public safety and democratic participation. But to have students play these roles effectively, the project needs stability and continuity in the administration of the three public schools included in the initiative—Futures Academy, Martin Luther King School (both K–8 schools), and East High School. Unfortunately, state and federal mandates are making that nearly impossible.

Let us take East High School, the one secondary school in the planning zone. Although East has had a rich history serving Buffalo's black community, producing many famous and accomplished graduates, recent years, as the East Side neighborhood has undergone disinvestment, depopulation, and decay in recent years, it has become a school of "last choice" in the Buffalo school district, and a revolving door for principals. Now, a brilliant new principal has been brought in who specializes in "turning around" tough schools and who is an enthusiastic partner in Professor Taylor's initiative. But as he told me when we met, the first day he entered the school he realized he would be out in three years because he could never raise graduation rates to meet national and state mandates. Why? Because of the 160 students in his freshman class, 157 were "1's" (on state reading and math tests), two were "2's, and one was a "3"! Essentially, *one* student in his freshmen class tested above grade level, and 157 students tested below!!

How did this happen? Basically, after magnet schools and charter schools picked their students, those who were left went to schools like East Side. Not only did these students test poorly, they disproportionately came from troubled families that moved from house to house with great frequency and occasionally disappeared. Given this population, it was going to be virtually impossible to meet the graduation rate targets established by the state and the school would (eventually) be placed in receivership, the principal removed, and up to 50 percent of the teachers replaced!

Given this tragic and absurd outcome, why did the principal take the job, and why did Dr. Taylor choose to make East High School one of the anchors of his community development initiative? Because they saw East students as more than the sum total of their scores on standardized tests and the problems they experienced in their homes and places of residence. They saw them as citizens in the making, possessed of invaluable knowledge about their neighborhood, and possessing a deep reservoir of cultural capital in artistic and musical talent, as well as resilience, endurance, and ability to overcome great obstacles. They wanted to incorporate them in the neighborhood planning process, get their frank assessments of what needed to be preserved and retained, and involve them in hands-on tasks ranging from cleaning up the local business district to organizing talent shows and oral history projects highlighting the community's past strengths and future potential. In the process, their test scores might go up, and attendance might improve. But these were not the major goals. The primary objective was to tap the full range of East students' talents in a process of community renewal, and encourage them to see East Buffalo as a place to be reimagined and rebuilt instead of human toxic waste site that all people with skill and talent seek to escape.

This kind of idealism and faith in the human potential of students and neighborhoods is at the very heart of what democratic education should be about. Unfortunately, it is being undermined, in the name of "equity," by federal and state policies that reduce students to test scores and graduation rates.

Dr. Taylor, the principal of East High School, and the principal of the other two schools in the East Buffalo Choice neighborhood initiative will persevere no matter what, but wouldn't it be better if state and federal authorities relaxed automatic school closing triggers and allowed schools the flexibility to become true centers of community empowerment? We can only hope that at some point, sanity will prevail in the US Department of Education and the New York State Board of Regents. Hopefully, that moment will come sooner rather than later.

THURSDAY, SEPTEMBER 8, 2011

The Bloomberg School Legacy: Flawed Policies Poisoned by a Fatal Arrogance

It should surprise no one that only 34 percent of New Yorkers approve of Michael Bloomberg's education policies, the policy area where the mayor most hoped to create a legacy. The mayor not only introduced numerous questionable initiatives—including school closings, preferential treatment of charter schools, and attempts to rate teacher performance based on student test scores—he did so with an arrogant disregard for the most experienced teachers and administrators in the system and also for parents, community leaders, and elected officials who tried to make their voices heard in matters of educational policy.

This top-down approach to reorganizing the city public school system not only reflected the ideology of the national school reform movement—

which viewed public schools as corrupt institutions in dire need of the kinds of competition and accountability allegedly characteristic of the private sector—but it was an egotistical effort to reproduce the success of Bloomberg LP by importing its management techniques into the Department of Education. For example, within weeks of taking office, the mayor put his mark on the school system by insisting the central headquarters of the New York City Department of Education, as well as all its district offices, look exactly like an office of Bloomberg Inc., with cubicles replacing offices. This astonishing reorganization, done without the input of anyone in the system, was designed to show that this mayor was determined to put his own personal stamp on the system down to the smallest detail, and a penchant for mayoral micromanagement has been a characteristic of the DOE ever since.

Among the highlights of mayoral micromanagement have been: 1) replacing four members of the Panel for Educational Policy, the major policy-making body governing the DOE, when they refused to base the promotion of third-graders exclusively on their performance of standardized tests; 2) publicly denouncing principals who questioned the school grades issued by the DOE after it became clear that the formulae used to compute those grades produced results that defied common sense; 3) appointing publishing executive Cathy Black as chancellor of the schools without the advice or input of anyone in the DOE, including outgoing chancellor Joel Klein; and 4) showing favoritism to charter school advocates who were personal friends, such as Harlem Success Academy director Eva Moskowitz, and giving them license to seize facilities from existing public schools, and discourage the enrollment by students who might lower their institution's test profiles.

It is one thing to try to convince educators and the public that schools, administrators, and teachers should be evaluated regularly on the basis of student test scores, and that public schools would benefit from competition from charters, it is another thing to implement those policies unilaterally, from the top down, while stifling public discussion and trying to browbeat and intimidate opponents.

Lost in the process were not only principles of democratic governance, but any kind of institutional check that would have subjected mayoral policies to external oversight or critical evaluation. Among the most damaging

results have been favoritism, cronyism, corruption in the awarding of Department of Education contracts, and the creation of evaluation systems, of schools and teachers that are wildly inaccurate and counterintuitive to what parents, teachers, and administrators believe.

When you have a system without checks and balances of any kind and without any institutionalized or marginally respected input from the major stakeholders in the system—parents, students, teachers, and administrators—don't be surprised if you generate tremendous opposition.

What we have now in New York is a school system filled with teachers and administrators working under extreme duress, convinced the mayor is their enemy, with students whose school experience is defined by one test after another, and with parents who feel their voices don't matter.

This is mayoral control Michael Bloomberg–style.

Many people in this city—teachers and principals foremost among them—will breathe a huge sigh of relief when his third term is finally up.

SATURDAY, AUGUST 20, 2011

School Reform, Community Development, and the Maldistribution of Wealth: The Road Not Taken

Reading Sarah Mosle's review of Steven Brill's new book on school reform in the *New York Times* reminded me of the incredible expenditure of time, money, and political capital this movement has engendered. I can think of no cause in recent American history that has brought together philanthropy, government, the media, and a bipartisan coalition encompassing elements of the Right and the Left in an effort to transform an important sector of American society. Using rhetoric that enlists egalitarian ideals (No Child Left Behind) alongside the goal of improving the nation's place in global capitalist competition (Race to the Top) this movement has proven well nigh irresistible in shaping the way educational policy is being formed at the state, local, and national levels.

Unfortunately, in terms of egalitarianism and competitiveness this movement has failed miserably. The nation become far more unequal in terms of every important statistical indicator (wealth distribution, youth poverty, minority unemployment, black/white wealth gap) since No Child Left behind was passed, and we have seen no change in the nation's position in the global hierarchy in terms of performance on standardized tests. Why has a movement that has inspired such elevated rhetoric ("education re-form is the civil rights cause of the twenty-first century"), such bipartisan political support, and such huge expenditures of money achieved so little? Perhaps the most obvious answer is a simple one: there is no evidence schools alone, no matter how well funded they are, can lift people out of poverty when every other social policy drives them down.

But that doesn't mean we should completely give up on transforming schools. Schools and school reform can serve as instruments of community development if the resources put into them are deployed in ways that strengthen local economies immediately, not just in some distant future when the beneficiaries of school reform graduate from college and launch successful careers.

Let's use a little imagination. What if the hundreds of billions of dollars contributed by philanthropists like Bill Gates, Eli Broad, and hedge fund entrepreneurs to charter schools, Teach for America, and local school dis-tricts who follow their model of "accountability" were used instead to hire local residents of poor communities to work in schools as school aides, recreation supervisors, and personnel in child care centers? Not only would such a policy help transform schools into dawn-to-dusk community centers for struggling neighborhoods, it would create tens if not hundreds of thou-sands of new jobs in neighborhoods that are starved for employment, and where families are under the severest economic stress.

Right now the vast majority of school reform dollars go into the pock-ets of middle-class and upper-middle-class professionals who live far from the neighborhoods in which "failing" schools are located—management consultants, employees of test companies, computer and information sys-tems managers, teachers and administrators in charter schools. They do nothing to develop local economies, strengthen families in need, provide employment to marginalized people, or redistribute income from the very wealthy to the very poor. If you wanted to be cynical, you can say that school reform, in the name of helping the poor, has created a wonderful job program for the children of the middle class. But that can only happen because most (but not all) school reformers divorce the goal of improving schools from the goal of lifting communities out of poverty.

As progressives, our job is to insist that the school/community linkage be foremost in all reform efforts, and that the vast majority of the funds to improve schools in poor communities are used to create jobs and programs for people who live in those communities. No more consultants, no more tests, no more computer systems, no more hotshot teachers who spend two years in low-performing schools then leave. Let's give bonuses to teachers and principals who live in the communities they teach in, stay in schools in poverty areas for ten or more years, and hire tens of thousands of local residents for useful and necessary work that turns schools into places where everyone in the neighborhood wants to be.

If you do that, you might not only contribute to the goal of greater equality, you will help put a dent in what all experts agree is the major hindrance to America's global competitiveness in educational performance—our extraordinarily high rate of child poverty.

THURSDAY, AUGUST 11, 2011
What I Would Do If I Had Arne Duncan's Job

First of all, I would state, for the record, that there is no quick or instant way to make our schools perform better unless we have a major initiative to reduce poverty that encompasses employment, health care, nutrition, housing, as well as education.

Then, I would end Race to the Top and No Child Left Behind, deemphasize standardized testing, and make schools places where young people, especially those from poor and working-class backgrounds want to spend time, and where they get skills that lead to useful employment. Here would be the keystones of my program:

1. Create first-rate vocational and technical education programs like those in Germany, and like those that existed in New York City in the 1950s. Help train the technicians needed to build a new energy-efficient economy for the twenty-first century.
2. Create after-school programs and night centers in the public schools that feature sports, the arts, and modern information technology, all led by teacher mentors, helped by teachers in training. Young people in New York City also had programs like these when I was growing up. They were eliminated during the 1970s fiscal crisis.
3. Vastly expand the hours and resources of public libraries so they create safe zones where young people can do their homework free of harassment and noise, and are places where they can have access to computer and information technology they might not have in their homes.
4. Create CCC- and WPA-type jobs program for out-of-work, out-of-school teens and young adults, paying them to help rebuild our rotting infrastructure and mentor young people in their neighborhoods.

I can assure you that these programs would be much more effective engaging young people than our current strategy of deluging them with standardized tests to make them "competitive" with young people in other countries.

MONDAY, AUGUST 1, 2011

The Lessons of History and the Save Our Schools March

The Save Our Schools Conference and March in Washington, DC, was the single most inspiring protest I have attended in the last thirty years. To see public school teachers from more than forty states rally in defense of their maligned profession, and hear the most important education scholars of our time tear apart the business/testing model driving education policy in the country, made me feel that I was part of a movement that was going to change school policies and reinvigorate justice organizing in a nation that had lost its way.

At the "Activism" panel at the Save Our Schools Conference, I had an epiphany that I want to share, not only with education activists but all people committed to progressive political change. It had to do with how we should relate to initiatives such as Teach for America and charter schools, which began with progressive missions but now are deluged with corporate money and seem to be committed to the business/testing paradigm that encourages privatization of public education and degrading the teaching profession.

My epiphany was this: if historic circumstances have moved these initiatives to the right, different historical circumstances can move them back to the left. And it could happen pretty quickly. If the current debt ceiling deal goes through, working-class and poor communities will suffer levels of hardship unseen in our lifetimes, making the prospect of schools, reformed or not, elevating people out of poverty seem improbable, if not absurd. Cuts in food support, housing grants, health care, youth recreation, and college access grants, all part of the debt reduction formula, are going to have heartrending effects on students in working-class communities, and put incredible pressure on every school and teacher in affected communities.

To think that Teach for America corps members and charter school teachers and administrators will be permanently immune to the rapidly escalating pain and hardship of students and families they work with defies common sense. Many will start to rethink the business/testing model of pedagogy they have been exposed to; some will become justice fighters for the communities they work within. And when that happens, progressives, whether in teachers unions or not, should be right there with them, encouraging them to participate in the broad struggle for democracy in America, and to use their positions as educators to help organize beleaguered communities to rise up and demand a fair share of the nation's wealth.

An impossible dream? Not really. Something like this happened seventy years ago during the heyday of the industrial labor movement. During the prosperous 1920s, the nation's largest corporations, including Ford

Motor Company, General Electric, and US Steel, organized company unions and employee representation plans to prevent their workers from joining trade unions. The strategy was so successful that no one major industrial corporation was unionized when the Depression struck.

But Depression conditions led to one-third of the labor force being unemployed and one-third working was part-time when Franklin Roosevelt assumed the presidency. This produced a rapid change in working-class attitudes. Organizers for industrial unions, largely ignored by workers during the 1920s, found workers receptive to their message in the three most important open-shot industries—steel, automobile, and electronics—and began to quietly infiltrate company unions. By the time the Congress of Industrial Organizations (CIO) was founded in 1935, company unions in the automobile and electronics industry began to affiliate en masse with the new CIO unions, giving them an immediate base in the heart of America's largest companies. The great sit-down strikes in the automobile industry, which led to the unionization of US Steel and well as General Motors, would not have happened had not company unions in the automobile industry become part of the CIO. The same dynamic occurred in the electrical industry, when Westinghouse and General Electric were organized by CIO unions.

Company unions, supported by the most powerful and wealthy corporations of that era, moved in a progressive direction in response to rapidly deteriorating economic conditions. There is no reason to assume that the same thing could not happen to charter schools and Teach for America in the coming years, as the American economy goes into free fall and working-class communities experience unspeakable hardships.

Given this, it behooves us as progressive organizers and justice fighters to keep lines of communication open to people in these organizations and be there to work with them if they join us in resistance to policies that concentrate economic sacrifice among America's poor.

Anything less than this would be selling our movement short. To stop the political juggernaut moving this nation to the right, we need to mobilize the broadest coalition of activists and organizers, including people we may have sharply disagreed with in the past.

FRIDAY, JULY 22, 2011

My Problem with Charter Schools? Too Many Are "Bad Neighborhood Citizens"

I am not in principle against charter schools. Experimenting with new models of school organization can be a good thing, and giving parents more options within the public school system can promote an atmosphere conducive to better teaching and learning. But in a society dominated by trickle-down economics, where there is little commitment to improve public education as a whole, charter schools have not fulfilled their original promise. With rare exceptions, they have functioned as though their success requires the failure of neighboring institutions. They have refused to work cooperatively with traditional public schools when they share a building; pushed out or excluded special needs, such as ELL [English Language Learner] children, and those marked as having "behavior problems"; and embraced what amounts to a two-tier system in inner-city schools, with one tier one favored and amply funded, and the other looked on with suspicion and contempt.

Charter schools can lead to improvements in the quality of education, but only if they embrace all children and try to work with and support public schools they share space and neighborhoods with, not quarantine them as if they were carriers of a contagious disease.

Right now, based on what I have seen in the Bronx and other parts of New York City, charter schools have not improved the quality of education in inner-city neighborhoods. The best have supplied a small number of families with better educational options. But on the whole, charter schools have been "bad neighborhood citizens," viewing everyone outside their ranks as a threat to their educational mission, and doing everything possible to "stack the deck" against traditional public schools by indirectly or overtly excluding students who might not test well or be compliant learners.

This "us against the neighborhood" is the last thing New York and the nation's immigrant and working-class communities need, as they find themselves starved of resources by budget cuts at the city, state, and federal levels.

Until charter schools start fighting for *all* the children and families in the neighborhoods they are located in, rather than the 10 percent enrolled in their institutions, they will be unable to make a positive contribution to the struggle for racial and economic equality in the United States.

NOTE: While there are some neighborhoods where 10 percent of students are enrolled in charter schools, in the nation as a whole, as Diane Ravitch points out, only 3.5 percent of students are in charter schools.

WEDNESDAY, JULY 6, 2011

Exposing Education Reform's Big Lie: It Is Jobs and Political Mobilization, Not Schools, That Lift People Out of Poverty

Once again, a major cheating scandal has been uncovered in an urban school district. What happened in Houston ten years ago (but not before its allegedly miraculous test score gains helped spawn No Child Left Behind) has happened in Atlanta. A state investigation has uncovered systematic falsification of test scores by teachers, principals, and district administrators in a district where careers could be made or broken by those results, and has led to the resignation of the district superintendent and potential suspensions. Scores of teachers and principals are facing possible criminal indictments.

To regard what took place in Atlanta as an exception to an otherwise unblemished record of probity in administering standardized tests would be like regarding Bernie Madoff's Ponzi scheme as an aberration in an otherwise healthy financial system. In each instance, unscrupulous individuals took the basic tenets of a flawed system to an extreme. In Madoff's case, he provided clients with high returns based on nonexistent investments rather than flawed ones (subprime mortgages packed into Triple-A bonds). In Atlanta, officials invented impossible results rather than brow-beating and terminating teachers and principals when they didn't achieve them.

Let us be clear—the Atlanta scandal is the logical outcome of a national movement, supported by government and private capital, to radically improve school performance and hopefully lift people out of poverty through a centrally imposed and rigidly administered combination of privatization, competition, material incentives, and high-stakes testing. You would think that a movement that commands such widespread support and extraordinary resources would have a history of proven examples, either in the United States, or other nations, to guide its implementation.

But the truth is that there has not been a single time in American history—with the exception of the ten years following the end of slavery—when educational reform was a factor that lifted a group out of poverty, or allowed a minority group to improve its status relative to the majority population. With that one exception of the Reconstruction Era during which activists founded schools for a people once denied literacy, the kind of "heavy lifting" required to do that has come not from top-down educational reform but from bottom-up political mobilization, coupled with changes in labor markets that have radically improved earning opportunities for the group in question.

Let us look at the one moment in the twentieth century where the African American population experienced a rapid improvement in its economic status and improved its status relative to whites, the time between 1940 and 1950. During those ten years, black per capita income rose from 44 percent of the white total to 57 percent, which meant that at a time when white per capita income was growing, black per capita income was growing even faster. This income growth was not only a result of wartime prosperity, and black migration from rural to urban areas, but a result of the protest movement launched by A. Philip Randolph in 1941 demanding equal treatment for blacks in the emerging war economy, and the enrollment of black workers in industrial unions. Randolph's march on Washington movement didn't lead to the desegregation of the armed forces, but it did lead President Roosevelt to issue a proclamation requiring nondiscriminatory employment in defense industries, and to create a commission to enforce this decree. While huge pockets of discrimination remained, African American men and women found work in factories throughout the nation producing ships, aircraft, and motorized vehicles, and joined unions that represented the bulk of workers involved in war production.

In Detroit, in Los Angeles, in Youngstown, in Pittsburgh, and in Richmond, California, black workers, many of them newly arrived in the South, were earning incomes four to five times what they would have made as sharecroppers or tenant farmers, and had union protection in their places of employment. This economic revolution spawned a political revolution, with nearly half a million African Americans joining the NAACP, and a cultural revolution as well. Rhythm and blues became the music of choice for the emerging black working class, inspiring clubs, radio stations, and small record labels to cater to this rapidly growing black consumer market. Though educational opportunities for blacks did improve in this period, it was changes in the job market, which had been fought for and consolidated by grassroots political movements, and reinforced by strong labor unions, that were the primary engine of change.

There is a lesson here that activists and educators should consider. If you want to improve economic conditions in black and working-class neighborhoods, then it would make more sense to raise incomes, either by unionizing low-wage industries or demanding that tax revenues be directed into job creation, than by legislating magical improvements in schools based on results on standardized tests.

Children living in impoverished communities cannot be miraculously vaulted into the middle class by pounding information into their heads and testing them on it relentlessly. However, their parents and older brothers and sisters can be lifted into the middle class through jobs that offer decent incomes and security, coupled with opportunities for personal advancement through education.

School reform is the American elite's preferred response to poverty and inequality, because it is a strategy that requires no sacrifice, no redistribution, or any self-organization by America's disfranchised groups. And every day, it is proving itself a dismal failure.

It's time that a new strategy be launched that focuses on jobs, economic opportunity, and the redistribution of wealth. We need a strategy linking civil rights groups, unions, and people living in working-class and poor communities who have watched wealth and opportunity be siphoned out of their communities by the very wealthy the same people, ironically, who are the biggest supporters of school reform!

WEDNESDAY, JUNE 22, 2011
Teach for America and Me: A Failed Courtship

Every spring without fail, a Teach for America (TFA) recruiter approaches me and asks if someone from the group can come to my classes and recruit students for TFA, and every year, without fail, I give her the same answer: "Sorry."

Until Teach for America changes its objective to training lifetime educators and raises the time commitment to five years rather than two, I will not allow TFA to recruit in my classes. The idea of sending talented students into schools in high-poverty areas and then, after two years, encouraging them to pursue careers in finance, law, and business in the hope that they will advocate for educational equity rubs me the wrong way.

It was not always thus. Ten years ago, when a Teach for America recruiter first approached me, I was enthusiastic about the idea of recruiting my most idealistic and talented students for work in high-poverty schools, and allowed the TFA representative to make presentations in my classes, which are filled with Urban Studies and African American Studies majors. Several of my best students applied. All of whom wanted to become teachers, and several of whom came from the kind of high-poverty neighborhoods TFA proposed to send its recruits to teach in.

Not one of them was accepted! Enraged, I did a little research and found that TFA had accepted only four of the nearly one hundred Fordham students who applied. I become even more enraged when I found out from the *New York Times* that TFA had accepted forty-four out of a hundred applicants from Yale that year. Something was really wrong here if an organization that wanted to serve low-income communities rejected every applicant from Fordham (many of whom came from those communities) and accepted al most half of the applicants from an Ivy League school (where very few of the students, even students of color, come from working-class or poor families). Since that time, the percentage of Fordham students accepted has marginally increased, but the organization has done little to win my confidence that it is seriously committed to recruiting people willing to make a lifetime commitment to teaching and administering schools in high-poverty areas.

Never in its recruiting literature has Teach for America described teaching as the most valuable professional choice that an idealistic, socially conscious person can make and encouraged the brightest students to make teaching their permanent career. Indeed, the organization does everything in its power to make joining Teach for America seem a like a great pathway to success in other, higher paying professions. Three years ago, the TFA recruiter plastered the Fordham campus with flyers that said, "Learn how joining TFA can help you gain admission to Stanford Business School." To me, the message of that flyer was "use teaching in high-poverty areas a stepping stone to a career in business." It was not only profoundly disrespectful of every person who chooses to commit her life to the teaching profession, it advocated using students in high-poverty areas as guinea pigs for an experiment in "resume padding" for ambitious young people.

In saying these things, let me make it clear that my quarrel is not with the many talented young people who join Teach for America. Some TFA educators of whom decide to remain in the communities they work in, and some become lifetime educators. Instead, it is with the leaders of the organization who enjoy the favor that TFA is regarded with by captains of industry, members of Congress, the media, and the foundation world. TFA leadership has used this access to move rapidly to positions as heads of local school systems, executives in charter school companies, and educational analysts in management consulting firms. The organization's facile circumvention of the grinding, difficult but profoundly empowering work of teaching and administering schools has created the illusion that there are quick fixes for failing schools and for deeply entrenched patterns of poverty and inequality. No organization has been more complicit than TFA in the demonization of teachers and teachers unions, and no organization has provided more "shock troops" for education reform strategies that emphasize privatization and high-stakes testing. Michelle Rhee, a TFA recruit, is the poster child for such policies, but she is hardly alone. Her counterparts can be found in New Orleans (where they led the movement toward a system dominated by charter schools); in New York (where they play an important role in the Bloomberg education bureaucracy); and in many other cities.

And that elusive goal of educational equity? How well has it advanced in the years TFA has been operating? Not only has there been little progress in the last fifteen years in narrowing the test score gaps by race and class, but income inequality has become greater in those years than at any time in modern American history. TFA has done nothing to promote income redistribution, reduce the size of the prison population, encourage social investment in high-poverty neighborhoods, or revitalize arts and science and history in the nation's schools. Its main accomplishment has been to marginally increase the number of talented people entering the teaching profession, but only a small fraction of those remain in the schools to which they were originally sent.

But the most objectionable aspect of Teach for America—other than its contempt for lifetime educators—is its willingness to create another pathway to wealth and power for those already privileged in the rapidly expanding educational-industrial complex by offering numerous careers for the ambitious and well connected. An organization that began by promoting idealism and educational equity has become, to all too many of its recruits, a vehicle for profiting from the misery of America's poor.

SUNDAY, MAY 22, 2011

The Money Trail in Education Reform Leads to Everyone But Those Who Need It the Most

In the last ten years, tens of billions of dollars have been spent to reform America's schools. Some of it has come from the Federal Department of Education, some of it from state legislatures, and some of it from private foundations. This money has gone to fund research on Common Core Standards; close failing schools and open up new ones; create new protocols for assessing schools and teachers; create new batteries of tests to evaluate students learning; bring management consultants into school systems and individual schools; and fund charter schools and educational maintenance organizations.

In New York City, education reform funding has spawned a variety of new public sector careers, ranging from "accountability officers" in the Department of Education and heads of charter school companies who make multiple six-figure salaries, to management consultants on the payroll of the DOE and scores of new principals whose jobs were created in small schools when large, allegedly "failing" ones were broken up. When you add to this the tens of millions of dollars spent to create new computer systems for the DOE, and the hundreds of millions of dollars given to publishing companies like McGraw-Hill to create new tests for almost every subject and every grade, you can see opportunities for profit making and career building this movement has inspired among aspiring professionals.

But how much of this funding has gone directly to the people this reform movement was supposedly created to help—working-class and minority students, and their families? How many jobs for students, or their parents, have education reform funds created, either in school programs or after-school centers? Has this money helped keep families in their apartments, allowed them to secure medical care or access better sports, arts, and recreation programs?

The answer to this is a resounding no. In New York City and around the nation, the funds have created a whole new layer of middle-class professionals in the schools—most of them white—and helped to create opportunities for profit for a number of private corporations, but have done nothing to ease the burden of poverty on the nation's working class and minorities.

As of 2011, the child poverty rate in the United States had reached 25 percent, the highest level since the Depression, and black unemployment had reached 16 percent. Given this, how can the supporters of test-driven education reform, whether they are in Washington, state houses, city halls, or the offices of major foundations, justify spending tens of billions of dollars to (allegedly) improve schools without one cent of it going into the pockets of poor people?

While people are losing their homes, their jobs, their medical care, their recreational opportunities, and are experiencing daily fear and stress, new school professionals are flooding their communities with programs that to date have offered no return on their investment to the people they were allegedly designed to benefit.

What we have in America, put forward by those who claim to put "Children First" is a cynical round of profit taking and career building reminiscent of the Gilded Age. It's time that people serious about ending poverty in America take a serious look at the education reform movement and *follow the money trail*! From what I can see, it leads directly into more profits for the haves and more hardship for the have-nots.

SATURDAY, MAY 14, 2011

Moment of National Insanity: Adding the Pressure of High-Stakes Testing to the Pressures of Poverty

Hearing that the governor of New York plans to raise student test scores from 20 percent to 40 percent of teacher ratings just reinforces my perception that a kind of insanity has overtaken those in charge of education in the United States.

The idea that we need to make passing standardized tests the central mission of our schools in order for the United States to remain competitive with other nations ignores the central role of imagination and creative thinking in the global economy, and is a strategy certain to increase the already immense economic disparities between the rich and poor in the United States.

In neighborhoods where young people need teachers to provide nurturing and support to counteract the harsh lives they often lead, tying teacher salaries and promotions to student performance on high-stakes tests will turn teachers into virtual slave drivers determined to squeeze results out of students lest their own jobs be in jeopardy. Where compassion and caring should prevail, this strategy builds in an adversarial relationship guaranteed to maximize stress on everyone involved.

As the film *Race to Nowhere* demonstrates, this can have negative consequences even in affluent communities, but the results will be most devastating to young people in poor communities who are alleged to be the primary beneficiaries of high-stakes testing. The last thing these young people need is for school to be turned into a zone of stress in which the teacher's job depends on students memorizing huge amounts of data, with no time left for art, music, play, or community-building activities.

Because to be poor in America is to live with stress. The stress of not knowing whether you will have enough food to get through the weekend without being hungry most of the time. The stress of not knowing whether the lights are going to get cut off, whether the heat will work, or whether you will be evicted from your apartment for nonpayment of rent, and forced to move to a shelter or taken in by relatives. The stress of living with fifteen people in a space meant for six, where you have to sleep in shifts, and where there is no place to do your homework. The stress of worrying whether your uncle, who you just moved in with, is going to sexually molest you or beat you up if you do something he doesn't like. The stress of having to go to the emergency room and wait eight hours for someone to see you. The stress of never being able to go to the dentist when you have a toothache. The stress of walking a gauntlet on your way to school, or even to the corner store, because someone doesn't like the way you look, the ethnic group you are part of, the block you live on, or because they think you are fair game for harassment because you are a young girl who has reached puberty. The stress of watching your mother get old before her time because she is working three jobs to keep you housed while being mistreated by bosses, husbands, boyfriends, and virtually every public servant she interacts with. The stress of being recruited for a gang and told that if you don't join, you will be made that gang's "bitch." The stress of being looked upon by every police officer as a potential criminal because you are a young person of color living in "the hood," and being stopped and searched by police with numbing regularity when you are doing nothing illegal.

So yes, let's take young people for whom those experiences are daily realities and ratchet up the pressure in school by increasing the number of tests they have, and telling teachers their careers are dependent on how those students perform on those tests.

Do you really think this is going to work? What you are going to do is push young people already near the breaking point over the edge. Some may obediently conform. But many more will rebel by lashing out at their teachers or their fellow students, or by leaving school to find some place they can find relief from the stress and pressure that is enveloping their lives.

Schools should be places where young people are nurtured, loved, and gradually given the skills to change their lives. It should be a safe zone, not a pressure cooker. Governor Cuomo is joining a long line of elected officials who, in the name of improving national competitiveness, are making a whole generation of young people—mostly but not all in poor and working-class neighborhoods—hate going to school. Our best teachers and principals know how damaging this is and are starting to speak out. But unless students and parents join the resistance to linking teacher evaluation to high-stakes testing, it will take years, possibly decades, to undo the damage that will be done to our schools by arrogant and misguided public officials.

MONDAY, MAY 9, 2011

If We Want to Rescue Our Public Schools—and Our Youth—It's Time to Start Teaching "Inequality"

All across the country, public school budgets are being cut. Teachers are being laid off, arts and sports programs are being eliminated, and class sizes are going through the roof. For working-class and immigrant youth, these policies mean that American society is no longer even promising them the illusion of social mobility. What awaits them, should they graduate from high school, is a grim choice between the military, low-wage labor, or immersion in the underground economy, coupled with the very real prospect of going to prison.

Given this grim reality, it is time for teachers to start reserving time in their classrooms to talk about the real story in America—inequality! Students in poor and working-class neighborhoods intuitively know that their futures are grim. Why not give them the evidence to show their suspicions are correct, and that policies can be adopted to give them greater opportunities if they are willing to organize and fight for decent-paying employment as well as a good education.

The best place to start your lesson plan is with income inequality. Every student in the United States should know that the top 1 percent of the population now controls 23 percent of the income, as compared to 9 percent in the 1950s and 1960s. Then move on to tax policy. Explain to students that the federal tax rate on the highest incomes, which was over 90 percent in the 1950s, is now below 40 percent. Then move on to union membership. Explain that in the 1950s, 35 percent of the American labor force were members of unions, as compared to 13 percent now. Conclude with the growth of the prison industrial complex. Explain that in 1980, less than four hundred thousand people were in federal and state prisons; there are more than two million people incarcerated today, and among African American males, there are now more people ages eighteen to thirty in prison than there are in college.

Then, after presenting these sobering statistics ask students to " connect the dots." Ask them if there is any relationship between income distribution and the growth of the prison population. Ask them to discuss who goes to prison, and how it affects those people's lives. Do people released from prison ever become part of the mainstream economy or are they permanently condemned to lives of poverty and insecurity? Ask students to write about people they know who went to prison and came out. What happened to those people? How did that experience affect their families?

Then move on to education. Have students analyze the education they are receiving. What kind of future are they being prepared for by a curriculum that puts so much emphasis on standardized tests? Ask them to compare the experience of people they know who graduated from high school and those who didn't. Was the experience of the two groups that different?

Then move on to politics. If the students conclude that the whole society, including the educational system, is stacked against them, what should they do about it? If they are going to protest, what examples in the past can be used as models? Teach them about the civil rights movement, the labor and unemployed movements in the Great Depression, the women's rights movement, and the movement against the war in Vietnam. Give them the example of the Greensboro lunch counter sit-ins when a group of four students decided to take history into their own hands. Ask them whether this protest has any relevance to what young people are going through today.

Then bring in hip-hop. Explain how hip-hop was created in the South Bronx by young people who had been written off by policy makers. They created an entire new musical form at the very same time that music programs, and music teachers, were removed from New York City schools. Ask them if that story, of marginalized young people making history, has any relevance to their experience. Ask them what it would mean for people like themselves to "make history."

The pedagogy I am describing, I guarantee you, will grab students' attention far more than the packaged history lessons being shoved down students' throats so they can pass standardized tests. It will also impart critical thinking skills, and encourage writing, reflection, and debate in manners that progressive educational reformers (those that still remain) would readily embrace.

But above all it would inspire students, many of whom now are deeply depressed and profoundly pessimistic, to see that they are not doomed to poverty and marginality, and that they can take actions to amplify their voices and change their circumstances.

Truth telling can be empowering. It can turn victims of unjust policies into agents of their own liberation. It is time for teachers to unleash the genie of "student power" through bold and inspired teaching.

SUNDAY, APRIL 3, 2011

Teaching Is Relationship Building—
Something School Reformers
Often Forget

One of the most pernicious examples of the tunnel vision of school reformers is the "school turnaround" concept incorporated in the Obama administration's "Race to the Top" legislation and currently being implemented in school districts throughout the nation. "Turnaround" strategy proposes that a school designated as "failing"—invariably based on test scores—be closed and either replaced with a charter school, or reopened as a new school in the same facility with a different principal and no more than 50 percent of the current teaching staff. Not only does this concept presume that "bad teachers" are the primary cause of a school's alleged failures, but it places no value on relationships that teachers build with students and their families. These relationships often last far beyond the time they were in class, are integral to student success, and help sustain teacher morale even in the most daunting conditions.

Anyone who has been a teacher knows that building up the confidence of students and giving them the courage to realize their potential and find their voices involves more than classroom learning. It often requires individualized instruction and mentoring, joint participation in extracurricular activities and trips, and a commitment to maintain communication long after the student leaves your class. When this happens, students come to see relationships with their teachers as sources of strength throughout their lives, as a form of "cultural capital" that allows them to surmount obstacles and realize their dreams.

In working-class and poor communities, where families are under constant stress, lifetime communication with teachers can be the critical factor enabling students to stay in school in the face of crises that would crush most people. Janet Mayer's wonderful new book, *As Bad as They Say: Three Decades of Teaching in the Bronx*, provides examples of how this longtime Bronx teacher supported her students through personal challenges that included evictions, murders, rapes, heatless homes, unemployed parents, and responsibilities for raising younger siblings.

This influence didn't just take place when students were in Mayer's classes. It often went on for fifteen or twenty years after they left her school. And students who could have easily fallen through the cracks became productive, successful citizens, some of choosing to become teachers themselves. The power of relationship building—which cannot be measured by student performance on standardized tests—is something I have experienced over and over again in my own teaching at the college level. The most transformative moments in my teaching have not taken place during class sessions, or on midterm or final examinations, but in individual encounters with students where they confront obstacles and implemented strategies to overcome them with my help.

An example, from the late '90s remains etched in my memory. M was a Fordham basketball star from an Irish working-class family in New Jersey, who had enrolled in several of my African American history classes with some of her teammates. She was incredibly shy, never saying a word in class, but one day, she showed up in my office and started crying. "Dr. Naison," she said, "I don't belong at this school. I only got 800 on my SATs and I feel like everyone here is so much smarter than me. What am I going to do?" I took a deep breath, prayed I wouldn't screw this up, and started developing a strategy. "M, they aren't smarter than you, they just have more educated parents and went to better high schools. But we are going to overcome that. Every time you write a paper, hand me a rough draft a week before and I will edit it for you. Before every test, come with your friends to my office and I will give you a strategy for studying as a group. And in return, you and your friends can work with me on my crossover and spin moves!" The last comment drew a reluctant smile from M and she went to work.

Little by little, she went from being a C student to a B student to getting B-pluses and A-minuses in the last class she took with me during the second semester of her senior year. But the best part of this transformation was watching M find her voice. By the time she graduated, she was not only participating regularly in class discussions, she was perceived as a leader by her fellow students, including those who came in to the school with much higher SAT scores and grades. After she graduated from Fordham M's confidence only grew. After playing pro basketball in Europe for several years, she returned to New Jersey and became a teacher and coach, using her own hard-won confidence to build the confidence of others.

In my forty years at Fordham, I have built many relationships with individual students I have taught, some of whom have gone on to become mayors of cities, leaders of government agencies, and world-renowned scholars and journalists, but no teaching or mentoring experience has been more satisfying than the one I had with M. Why? Because M represents the majority of students attending schools in America's poor and working-class communities. They not only lack the skills that upper-middle-class students acquire in their families and the high-performing schools they attend, they often suffer from a crippling lack of self-confidence in approaching school tasks.

That confidence deficit, I am convinced, is at least as important as the skills deficit, and it cannot be overcome through test-prep drills and group instruction. It requires individual attention from teachers, and not just in a classroom setting. It requires extra work and encouragement after school, on weekends, and sometimes long after the student leaves the teacher's direct care. If you rotate teachers in and out of schools at a dizzying rate and create pressures that drive them out of the profession after a few years, you will destroy the relationship-building component that is at the heart of great teaching. Ironically, under the pressure of federal mandates, this is being done in the very communities that have the greatest needs for inspired teaching and mentoring.

THURSDAY, MARCH 3, 2011

How Public School Budget Cuts Herald the End of Equality in the United States—Even as an Ideal

Throughout the United States, the nation's public school system is being savaged by budget cuts that will make a mockery of federal legislation designed to reduce the achievement gap between children in low-income and high-income districts.

In Detroit, the school district has been told by the state to close half of its schools to reduce a $347 million deficit, leading to high school classes that could contain as many as sixty students. Schools in Providence, Rhode Island just handed out pink slips to nearly two thousand teachers to reduce its deficit; Austin, Texas, may do the same in a response to a 10 percent reduction in state funding. And in thousands of school districts throughout the country teachers are being fired, sports and arts programs are being shut down, AP classes are being cancelled, and class sizes are going through the roof while state and local governments radically cut education funding to balance their budgets.

Make no mistake about it, these budget cuts will have a disproportionate effect in the poorest school districts, where parents depend on schools to impart skills because of educational background or language issues they often lack. If arts and science programs are eliminated in an upper-middle-class school district, parents can compensate by finding private tutors or funding additional classes through the PTA. In poor neighborhoods, once such programs are gone, they are gone for good. You can squeeze the teachers in poor districts all you want to produce magical results on test days, but as opportunities to give students individual attention and special training in arts and science disappear, the test score gap will grow wider, the dropout rate will increase, and college admission rates in these districts will plummet.

What makes this a bitter pill to swallow is that the dream these budget cuts will destroy was nurtured by a Republican president, George W. Bush. Never mind that the dream was based on false data from the Houston school district, never mind that it was used by politicians, business leaders, and the media to divert attention from confronting sources of inequality outside the school system. Every child in America had the right to a great education and an opportunity to attend college if they took advantage of that opportunity.

Now this dream is in tatters, not just because of decisions to cut public school budgets, but because of a decision politicians didn't make: to *tax the rich*. Make no mistake about it—in each state where these budget cuts are being made, the most reductions could have been avoided if taxes were raised on the wealthiest five percent of the population, who control nearly 40 percent of national income! Yet in state after state, as well as in the Congress of the United States, such taxes were declared "off limits" by politicians in both parties.

Let us be very blunt about the consequences of this choice. In the midst of the worst economic crisis in modern US history, our political leadership has decided to exempt the very wealthy from sacrifice while tragically weakening the one avenue our society had identified for reducing inequality in the nation—our public schools. Not only is it profoundly immoral to impose hardship on the weakest and most vulnerable members of our society, targeting schools for such huge cuts does violence to the very ideal of equality of opportunity that once used to unite liberals and conservatives.

If the only schools that can function well are in communities where parents have the resources to compensate for the budget cuts, then we are creating a social order where children will retain the social class of their parents into the next generation, and where poor and working-class children are doomed by inferior training to be servants for the rich, if they are lucky enough to find jobs at all.

I don't know about you, but this sounds more like the Old Order in France or prerevolutionary Russia than the country that Abraham Lincoln once praised "for lifting artificial burdens off the shoulders of men."

The American Dream is dying before our eyes. Will we have the courage to rescue it?

Sunday, January 29, 2012

How a Crackpot Education Reform Theory Became National Policy

In future generations, historians are likely to tell the following story. Sometime during the early twenty-first century, a cross section of the top leadership of American society began to panic. They looked at the growing chasm between the rich and poor, the huge size of the nation's prison population, the growing gulfs in educational achievement between blacks and whites and between poor and middle-class children, and decided something dramatic had to be done to remedy these problems.

But instead of critically examining how these trends reflected twenty years of regressive taxation, a futile "war on drugs," the deregulation of the financial industry, the breaking of unions and the movement of American companies abroad, America's leaders decided the primary source of economic inequality could be found in failing schools, bad teachers, and powerful teachers unions.

No serious scholar looking at the economic and social trends of the previous twenty years, or the major innovations in social policy that unleashed the power of big capital, would have given the slightest credence to this analysis of the sources of inequality. But the idea that educational failure was the prime source of all other social deficits took hold with the force of a religious conversion. Corporate leaders, heads of major foundations, civil rights leaders, politicians in both major parties, bought this explanation hook, line, and sinker, and so began one of the strangest social movements in modern American history—the demonization of America's teachers and the development of strategies to radically transform education by taking power away from them.

The consequence of this leap of faith, supported by no serious research, was the idea that there has to be centralized efforts to monitor educational progress though quantifiable measures coupled with accountability strategies calling for the removal of teachers and the closing of schools if they didn't meet certain criteria. Through policies developed at the federal level, but implemented locally so that they affected every school district in the nation, scrutinizing teacher effectiveness became a national mission introduced with as much fanfare as America's efforts to put a rocket in space during the 1950s and '60s.

The centerpiece of this mission was that teachers had to be judged on student performance on standardized tests, as there were no other "objective" criteria that could generate meaningful statistical information on a national scale. But America's states and municipalities did not have consistent testing policies, so federal policies called for universal testing related to a nationally developed set of Common Core Standards, with the loss of federal funding being presented as the consequence of failure to comply.

This all sounds very rational until you look at it from the individual school level. To evaluate teachers via standardized tests, and to do it across the board, you have to have tests in every grade and every subject. This not only means tests in English, math, science, and social studies, it means tests in art, music, and gym.

No school in any country, at any time in history, ever tried doing something like this, and for good reason. It means that all that goes on in school is preparation for tests. There is no spontaneity, no creativity, no possibility of responding to new opportunities for learning that relate to events that occur locally, nationally, or globally. It also means play and pleasure are erased from the school experience and students are put under constant stress, maximized by teachers who know that their own job security depends on student performance.

What you have here, in short, is a prescription for making the nation's schools a place of fear and dread, ruled by test protocols that deaden minds and stifle creative thinking. There are people who stand to benefit handsomely from this insanity, especially the companies who make the tests and the consultants who administer them, but anyone who thinks this level of testing will make America's schools more effective or reduce social inequality has a capacity for self-delusion that staggers the imagination. Only people with no options would choose to send their children to schools run that way. The wealthy will send their children to private schools that eschew testing, and the well-organized will withdraw from the system to create their own cooperative schools or engage in home schooling.

The sad part about all of this is that the Obama administration, like the Bush administration, continues to push this program with the support of both major parties and a cross section of America's corporate leadership.

There are not too many other examples in American history where such a crackpot theory guided social policy this way. The last example I can think of was the passage of the Prohibition Amendment to the US Constitution, based on the conviction that banning alcoholic beverages would somehow create greater social stability and save America from corruption.

Some day, test-based education reform will go the way of Prohibition. But not before incalculable damage is done to the nation's children.

Press Release about Educators Letter to President Obama and Campaign to Remove Arne Duncan as Secretary of Education

For Immediate Release
February 5, 2012

A Letter to President Obama

Two grandparents on opposite ends of the continent each had a concern about the direction of education reform and its effect on their grandchildren. Through a chain of improbable circumstances they found each other on Facebook and conjured up a letter to President Obama expressing their concerns.

Mark Naison, from Brooklyn, New York, and a Fordham professor prepared a draft of the letter. Bob Valiant, retired school administrator from Kennewick, Washington, edited the letter and Bob Valiant Jr. developed a survey form and website http://dumpduncan.org/. The letter calls for the removal of Education Secretary Arne Duncan and the inclusion of parents, teachers, and school administrators in all administration policy discussions. It insists on the immediate end to penalties and incentives to compel use of student test scores to evaluate teachers, require school closures, or install charter schools. Finally, the letter asks for a national commission, to include parents and teachers, to explore ways to improve the public schools.

Naison and Valiant Sr. began to circulate the letter to friends on Facebook on February 3, 2012. The signatures started rolling in, and by the start of the Super Bowl on February 12 more than 2,000 total signatures had been recorded. A map on the website shows they came from all across the country, from big cities, suburbs, and hamlets. All of this happened with a purely volunteer cadre made up of parents, teachers, and other concerned citizens with no financial expenditure. Now the goal is to continue collecting signatures until March 1 when the letter and package of signatures will be delivered to the president.

For further information, consult the website http://dumpduncan.org.

Help ensure the long-term survival of the greatest public education system on Earth by signing this open letter to President Obama.

SUNDAY, FEBRUARY 6, 2011

What's Love Got to Do with It? Is Test-Driven Educational Reform Driving the Joy in Learning from the Nation's Classrooms?

Sometime during my childhood, probably before the age of eight, I fell in love with learning new things. Maybe it was the trips to the Bronx Zoo and the American Museum of Natural History I took with my parents, maybe it was the explosions I made with my chemistry set (which today would mark me off as a future terrorist!). Maybe it was the wonder of reading about dinosaurs and how humans and modern apes had common ancestors. Maybe it was the excitement of memorizing the capitals of every state and the batting averages of major league players. But I became a person to whom the joy of acquiring and making sense of new information was as powerful as my love of food, sports, and music.

The public schools I went to, though students sat in rows and did more than their share of memorization, did much to encourage the intellectual curiosity of kids like me. There were science fairs and spelling bees, regular trips to zoos and museums, science labs, arts projects, and an audio-visual squad that allowed its student members, once they were properly trained, to show films for the entire school. There were assemblies where we sang and put on plays, regular recess where we played punch ball and Johnny-on-the-Pony, and gym classes where we did calisthenics and played dodge ball. Sure, there were fights with tough kids and bad moments with mean teachers—and I had my share of both—but I loved going to school. So much so that I became a teacher myself, figuring that the best way to keep the joy of learning alive was to share it with future generations of students.

Today, with all the pressure on students to pass standardized tests, and the public humiliation and possible loss of jobs awaiting principals if their students don't "perform," I wonder if students who grew up in working-class neighborhoods like mine (Crown Heights, Brooklyn) are having the love of learning smothered and driven out of them in the schools they are attending? The feedback I am getting from my former students who teach in such schools is not encouraging. Huge amounts of their teaching time is devoted to test preparation, and they are under close and constant scrutiny by school administrators whose own careers are now entirely dependent on student performance. More and more, the principal becomes like a high-level college coach whose future employment depends on their win-loss percentage, and they pass that pressure on to their teachers and students as surely as those coaches do to their players. What disappears in that situation is joy—joy in playing, joy in learning, joy in teaching. Young people who should be experiencing the wonder of discovery are being told, in ways indirect and direct, that the jobs of the teachers and administrators who work with them are dependent on their performance on the tests they are taking. No young person should be subjected to that kind of pressure at age eighteen, much less at age eight! What you have is a situation where the time and space for creative playful thinking and experiential learning is being squeezed out of the school culture. School is no longer a place for dreamers, for adventurers, for people who live in a world of the imagination. It is a place for people who dutifully follow orders and respond to a fear of failure.

Unfortunately, things have gotten much worse since Barack Obama took office and launched Race to the Top. Seven years ago, a visionary school leader, Julia Swann, invited me into thirteen Bronx elementary schools and middle schools to train teachers to do oral and community history projects with their students. Ms. Swann had located a two-month window of opportunity in the school year when teachers were no longer under pressure to do "test prep," and she thought that community history projects would be something that would energize school communities and get parents more involved in the schools.

Ms. Swann's vision proved prophetic! The teachers leaped on the opportunity to bring the history of Bronx neighborhoods to life in the classroom. Students interviewed their parents and grandparents, their teachers, and neighborhood merchants and created amazing visual as well as literary records of what they had learned. Some schools had daylong oral history festivals and invited the entire neighborhood, and these events featured poster board displays, exhibits (some of near-museum quality), journals and newspapers, performances, student-made documentary films, and food fairs highlighting the cuisines of the various cultural groups represented in the school. One school, PS 140 in Morrisania, created an "old school museum" honoring the cultural and musical traditions of the neighborhood and decided to make community history an integral part of the school culture. Everywhere I went (and I attended events at all thirteen schools!) I saw incredible joy on the faces of teachers, students, parents, and administrators when they showcased what they had done. There was no pressure to meet an external standard, or pass muster with an outside reviewer. Rather, there was the joy of discovering that history lived right among them, in the stories told by the people closest to them, and in the material objects (immigration records, birth certificates, articles of clothing, recipes, records, and tapes) that they had preserved. I even wrote a little rap, which I performed at all thirteen schools, to honor what had taken place:

Region 2 and Network 3
Are Rocking Oral History
Our 13 schools, in the BX
Are using daily life as text

We do food, music, and immigration
To show how the Bronx leads the Nation
With hip-hop, salsa, and R and B
The Mixing of Cultures is Our Family Tree

Working on this project, with these remarkable Bronx students, teachers, and administrators, may have been the best single experience in my forty years as a college teacher. Unfortunately, it could never be done today. Why? Because there is no longer a two-month period in the school year when teachers are free of the pressure of test prep! Now, you are lucky if you could find a *week* in which classroom learning is not dominated by the pressure of student, teacher, and school evaluation.

This, to me, is a crime. Not against the children of the wealthy, who go to private schools, or suburban public schools, where the arts and science and creative learning are still integral to the school experience, but to working-class kids like I once was who are filled with intellectual curiosity, but are having the joy in learning replaced by pressure and stress passed down relentlessly from school administrators to teachers to children.

Make no mistake about it, when we destroy the joy of learning in a large portion of our youth, most of whom are racial minorities and from immigrant backgrounds, we are doing our nation irreparable harm.

Will people please wake up and stop this travesty against the young people of our nation? Let students learn, let teachers teach, let the joy return to our schools.

MONDAY, DECEMBER 3, 2012
Hope for Embattled Educators

This is a daunting time to be a teacher in the United States of America. At work, almost every day brings word of a new test, a new assessment, a new rubric for accountability that makes teachers and students jump through another hoop. Media and elected officials add to the stress and anxiety. Public declarations of devotion to the cause of "education reform," which teachers have learned to interpret as attacks on their professional integrity, and are commonplace, to create opportunities blame teachers for the nation's failure to be competitive on international tests, or reduce poverty and inequality. But worst of all is the scripting of the classroom environment by testing and technology in ways that eliminate the spontaneity that makes teaching fun, and the relationship-building that makes teaching meaningful. The classroom has become a zone of surveillance, and it is not too farfetched to imagine that video cameras will eventually be installed to make sure teachers are not deviating from the curricula that have been purchased to insure good results on the tests that have been imposed.

In the short run, there may be no way to stop this. Too many people have built careers on promoting these "reforms," and too many people are making money implementing them. But little by little, those on the receiving end of these initiatives—whether they are teachers, school administrators, students, or parents—are feeling discouraged, smothered, humiliated, and abused. Uncontrolled proliferation of testing, which now begins in pre-K, and is rapidly extending to subjects like art, music, and gym, has made school so boring and stress-filled that the people in it are experiencing clinical systems of anxiety and depression. And that is among the "successful"! Special needs students, ELL students, and those whose lives are so unstable they can't give learning their full attention, are being subjected to a form of "educational triage" startling in its cruelty, lest they pull down test scores and subject everyone else to awful penalties—which can include closing of schools and mass firing of teachers!

In response, a simmering rage has begun to manifest itself among those most affected. It began with conversations, most of them private; then meetings; then formation of organizations; then rallies, marches, boycotts, lawsuits, and strikes—the same model followed by movements of the sixties on behalf of women's and gay rights. While these movements—Save Our Schools, United Opt Out, Dump Duncan, Parents Across America, the Chicago Teachers strike—are still in their early stages, and have not stopped the education reform juggernaut, they have robbed it of its air of romance, exposed its links to big money interests, and challenged its claim to promote the cause of equity and civil rights. Most importantly, they have let individual teachers, parents, and students feeling smothered and abused by the new policies know that they are not alone and that resistance is possible.

While it is impossible at this stage to know whether these resistance movements will be strong enough to force political leaders to withdraw their support from privatization and testing, they have created enough of a grassroots presence to publicly challenge and contest almost every reform initiative at the local and national level. We now have a counter narrative, based on strong scholarship as well as experience that warns that reform policies are likely to widen educational disparities rooted in race and class and weaken the nation's schools by driving out the most committed teachers. And people are listening. An extravagantly funded Hollywood film, *Won't Back Down*, supporting a favorite reform cause—parent trigger legislation—got so little public support it was judged one of the greatest failures in the history of Hollywood film. A rally in New York City in support of teacher assessments based on standardized tests, organized by Students for Education Reform chapters at NYU and Columbia, was a dismal failure. Parent trigger legislation and charter school initiatives have been voted down in several states, and parents across the country are filing lawsuits protesting the impact of test mandates on special needs students.

The reform agenda is backed by limitless money and is fueled by the profit motive as well as political ambition, but because it turns schools into zones of fear and stress, the best it can do is compel opportunistic implementation and sullen compliance. And as teachers, students, and parents step forward to say that our nation can and must do better than deluging schools with unnecessary tests, their courage and their patience will eventually inspire a moral and political awakening that will force policy makers and the media to take notice.

The first step is telling the truth about what reform is really doing to our schools; the second step is to share that insight with colleagues, friends, and family; the third step is to attend rallies and public meetings that challenge the reform agenda; and the fourth step is to opt out, boycott, strike, and sue.

Most of us are still in stages one and two, but because reformers have no shame and believe their own propaganda, they will continue to impose an agenda so manifestly ill-conceived and self-destructive that it will force more and more people into open rebellion. In the service of this revolt, I proclaim the following:

Testing Is Not Teaching
You Can't Improve School Performance by Making Children Hate School
Demoralizing Teachers and Principals Doesn't Make Schools Better
Let's do this people. We have nothing to lose but our assessments!

School Closings and Public Policy: The Anatomy of a Catastrophe

The threat of school closings which hang over Chicago public schools has been a central feature of Bloomberg educational policies in New York, and are perhaps the most controversial consequence of the Obama administration's Race to the Top initiative. The idea of closing low-performing schools, designated entirely on the basis of student test scores, removing half of their teaching staff and all of their administrators, and replacing them with new schools—often charters—in the same building, has tremendous appeal among business leaders, and almost none among educators.

Advocates see this policy as a way of removing ineffective teachers, adding competition to what had been a stagnant sphere of public service, and putting pressure on teachers in high-poverty areas to demand and get high performance from their students, once again based on performance on standardized tests.

For a "data-driven" initiative, school closings have produced surprisingly little data to support their implementation. In New York City, there has been no perceptible decline in test score gaps between black, Latino, white, and Asian students, since the school closings were initiated (even though more than 140 schools in the city have been closed). More tellingly, the percentage of black and Latino students in the city's specialized high schools, admission to which are based entirely on test scores, is the lowest in the city's history, prompting a lawsuit from the NAACP.

But opposition to closings is not just based on lack of "hard" evidence to support their implementation. It is based on three broadly observed consequences of the closings: their propensity to ignore the voices of students, parents, and teachers and ride roughshod over the democratic process; their creation of pressures that transform teaching into test prep and lead to the elimination of art, music, physical education, and school trips; and the destabilizing of already wounded neighborhoods by undermining relationships between schools, communities, teaching staffs, and families.

In New York City, where school closings have been public policy for more than four years, I don't know of an example of parents and students mobilizing to demand the closing of a troubled school, but I do know many instances where they have mobilized to oppose school closings. With few exceptions their voices have been ignored by the Panel for Educational Policy, the Bloomberg-controlled arbiter of school closing decisions. Test scores and Department of Education recommendations have ruled the day. With the elimination of local school boards and the imposition of mayoral control, there is no institutional channel with power to represent community interests. Children and parents are being given a devastating lesson here—that their voices don't count. Only those who think the goal of public education is to create a passive, disciplined, labor force willing to accept any work offered to them should take comfort in this.

A second consequence, even more devastating, is how the threat of school closings ratchets up stress levels in low-performing schools. This has led to epidemics of clinical depression among teachers and stress-related disorders in children, and it led many schools to drastically transform their curricula to assure students pass tests. First to go are art, music, hands-on science, and school trips; there have also been many instances of gym, recess, and after-school programs being reduced to make room for test prep, which magnifies already serious obesity problems among children in places like the Bronx where there is little access to healthy food, and few out-of-school opportunities for regular exercise. The conditions I have described, in some schools, have reached levels that could best be described as child and teacher abuse. It is time that those making these policies take responsibility for what happens when schools close, and for the pedagogy that schools in high-poverty neighborhoods implement to assure that they won't be closed.

Finally, there is the issue of neighborhood stability. In poor neighborhoods, it is common for young people to move from household to household—sometimes from household to shelter—in response to the economic instability of their caregivers. Many children are being brought up by grandparents or other relatives; some are in foster care, some are homeless. In this situation, schools are often the main point of stability in children's lives and teachers' important mentors. I know of many teachers in such communities who financially support their students, take them on trips, and sometimes have them come to their homes on weekends. Closing schools and removing teachers undermines the critical community-building function of public schools, leaving young people without important anchors in their lives. Given this, no one should be surprised by rising levels of violence in communities where this policy is being applied. We need schools in such communities to be safe zones, not places of fear and dread where everyone involved is waiting for the hammer to fall based on the word of someone downtown who has no idea what people in the neighborhoods are living through, or who just doesn't care.

I urge all who have read this piece to think very carefully whether school closings are instruments to promote greater equity, or whether they intensify the problems they were meant to remedy, and create new problems in their wake.

MONDAY, OCTOBER 1, 2012

Letter to Maggie Gyllenhaal re: Won't Back Down

Just posted this on Maggie Gyllenhaal's fan page on Facebook:

I regret to say that you have lost the respect of many people who admired you by not only taking a role in *Won't Back Down*, but by defending the movie's message. It pains me a great deal to say this, because I knew your mother when we were both in college, and because you spoke at an art auction for the school where my wife Liz is principal, but taking in a role in a film financed by Philip Anschutz and supporting legislation supported by the American Legislative Exchange Council, is something that no progressive person I know can understand. Worse yet, your movie has made teachers around the country feel more embattled, more attacked, at a time when teacher morale is the lowest in recorded history. This is a time when people of conscience should be standing with teachers against powerful interests who are trying to privatize our public education. Unfortunately, you have stood with the billionaires against the teachers, while seeming to speak on behalf of parents. The only hope for public education is for parents and teachers to unite as they did in the Chicago Teachers strike. Supporting parent trigger legislation, which pits parents against teachers, is exactly the wrong move at this historic moment. Please tell your mother, Naomi, what I just said. And tell her to contact me if she wants to talk.

FRIDAY, SEPTEMBER 7, 2012

Stubborn Facts About Obama Education Policies That No Amount of Convention Sugarcoating Can Cover Up

If you watched the Democratic Convention, you would never know that the Obama administration's education policies were extremely controversial with America's teachers, and had provoked outrage among many of the nation's most distinguished education scholars. Chicago mayor Rahm Emmanuel spoke at the convention without anyone mentioning that his policies had provoked an impending strike among tens of thousands of teachers, and that these policies were supported by the administration's secretary of education Arne Duncan.

Duncan also spoke at the convention, making the incredible statement that "no teacher should teach to the test" when his Race to the Top policies require that teacher evaluations be partially based on student test scores. Of course, this has resulted in "teaching to the test" everywhere those funds distributed. And finally, the president's statement that "teachers shouldn't be fired" goes squarely against the school-closing component of Race to the Top, which mandates that schools designated as failing (again by the criterion of test scores), should be closed, and that 50 percent of teaching staffs removed.

What was also not said is that the Obama education policies are the one part of its political program most praised by Republicans, and that Obama officials have effusively praised the education policies of two Republican governors, Jeb Bush and Chris Christie. Because these policies are likely to be continued no matter which party wins the presidency, it is important to enumerate some of the negative consequences of the Race to the Top initiative that has been a hallmark of this administration.

The following are some stubborn facts about the consequences of Obama administration education policy everyone should be aware of. Fact one: Teacher morale is at the lowest level it has been in recorded history. This is, in part, because virtually every major leadership group in society has blamed teachers for the nation's problems, and also because teachers' job protections and job rights are under attack as they are increasingly evaluated on the basis of student test scores. Fact two: special needs students and ELL students are everywhere experiencing humiliation, and occasionally outright discrimination, because students who do not test well are seen as threatening the careers of teachers and school administrators. It is in the interest of schools to exclude such students or push them out to maintain a positive test profile, a practice notoriously common among some of the nation's best-known charter schools. Fact three: the teaching force in the nation is being steadily "whitened" as a result of school closings and teacher firings mandated by Race to the Top, and by the replacement of experienced union teachers in large city school districts with Teach for America corps members. Fact four: students throughout the country, even in middle-class, high-performing districts, are increasingly complaining that they hate school because of an enormous rise in the number and frequency of standardized tests and the elimination of gym, recess, sports, and the arts to make room for test prep.

These problems will all intensify in coming years unless there is a radical change in the nation's education policies. Based on what transpired at the Democratic Convention, no such change will be forthcoming unless there is something close to a revolt on the part of America's teachers, students, and parents.

TUESDAY, SEPTEMBER 11, 2012

Chicago's Teachers "Won't Back Down" and Inspire Teachers Throughout the Nation

Whatever the outcome, the Chicago Teachers strike shows that a broad section of the nation's teachers are fed up with being made whipping boys for the nation's failure to reduce racial and economic inequality, and to provide equal educational opportunity for its citizens. You do not mobilize tens of thousands of people to put their jobs at risk and take to the picket line unless there is a powerful undercurrent of frustration and rage with the way they have been treated. The strike won't stop education reformers—who have the support of the nation's biggest corporations—from cementing their stranglehold on education policy on the local and national level, and from consolidating their influence in both major parties. But it pulls aside the facade of support and compliance with the Obama administration's education policies that the Democratic National Convention hoped to project, and revealed how wildly unpopular Race to the Top is with many of America's teachers, and a small, politically savvy group of public school parents. The strike also provides a powerful antidote to the propaganda campaign for the new Hollywood teacher-bashing movie *Won't Back Down*, which hits American theaters at the end of the month. The sea of red shirts marching through Chicago, and the teachers around the country wearing red in solidarity, show that teachers may not be as easy a target as the movie's backers anticipated.

The Chicago Teachers Union has flipped the script on Michelle Rhee, Democrats for Education Reform, and other backers of school privatization and showed how a teachers union can be a militant advocate for the right of students to have a school experience that includes music, art, sports, and class sizes small enough to receive individual attention. There is no guarantee that the strike will achieve its major goals, but it has already succeeded in giving America's teachers a huge emotional lift and in forcing the media to recognize that teachers' voices cannot be marginalized and suppressed without significant consequences.

Message to My Teacher Friends at the Start of a New School Year

The start of a new school year is normally an exciting time. Teachers are busy decorating their classrooms, preparing their lessons, reconnecting with colleagues, imagining what they are going to say that first day when they meet their students. But this year, teachers will have many other things on their minds. We live in a society where every important group—politicians, business leaders, media pundits, even Hollywood film personalities—is quick to blame teachers, not only for the alleged failures of our schools, but the failure of our society to reduce poverty and inequality. If that public demonization isn't enough, almost every public school system in the nation is engaging in experiments in behavior modification using teachers as guinea pigs, rating teachers on the basis of students' test scores, deluging their classrooms with consultants, and promising to reward them for improved student performance or fire them if they fail to produce it. Not only do these strategies turn the classroom into a zone of continuous stress, they create adversarial relationships between teachers and students, teachers and parents, and between teachers in the same school whose performances are rated against one another.

As the child of two public school teachers, the husband of a public school principal, and scholar who has spent a great deal of time in Bronx schools working with teachers on community history projects, I am enraged by these policies. And I am here to tell you this: The very fact that you continue to work and serve your students under these conditions makes you our nation's unsung heroes! Because you understand something that the billionaires and econometricians shaping education policy won't recognize— that the magic in the classroom, whether it comes in the form of teaching someone to read, nurturing a musical or artistic skill, or inspiring someone to do research on their family or community, comes from connecting with individual children, and not by sticking to a prepackaged formula.

And connecting with those children means appreciating everything they bring to the classroom, some of which might make learning harder, some of which might be the key to inspiring them. It is making this connection, sometimes in the face of what seems like insuperable odds, that keeps teachers up at night and wakes them up in the morning fired up with enthusiasm and determination. Those who rate you and measure you, those who hold you up to ridicule, those who seek to turn parents and the general public against you, have no conception of the emotions that teaching involves or the pride you feel when you get through to young people and give them the confidence to do things they thought were beyond them. I would say "forgive them, for they know not what they do," but that isn't entirely true. All too many of the people attacking you and telling you how to do your jobs are doing so for narrow personal gain, either because they think it will help them get elected, or they hope to profit from privatizing what was once a public trust. But in spite of the forces arrayed against you, do not give up or give in, because you are all that stands in between our children dehumanization.

There is no metric that can measure love. There is no metric that can measure compassion. There is no metric that can measure imagination. There is no metric that can measure humor. You are our hope. You are our future. Stay true, stay strong. Someday the nation will recognize that your vision and your best practices are the only sure path to improving our schools.

THURSDAY, JULY 12, 2012

Education and Trickle-Down Segregation in Michael Bloomberg's New York

The other day, I was walking to an appointment on East 125th Street in Harlem and saw an interesting sight outside the huge new building housing Promise Academy, the central institution of Geoffrey Canada's much-celebrated Harlem Children's Zone. A teacher was marching about twenty children from one entrance in the building to another. All twenty children were black, dressed in uniforms of white blouses with blue trousers or skirts, and they moved through the street with discipline and purpose. This was the face of one of the city's best-known charter schools. I could not help but contrast it with a scene I regularly see outside PS 107 on Eighth Avenue between Thirteenth and Fourteenth Streets in Park Slope when I drive by the school. There, on a typical late morning or early afternoon, I see groups of parents, virtually all white, taking their children to school or picking them up, their movements cheerful and often chaotic. The whiteness of the group never fails to stun me because in the '80s, when my friends' kids went there, PS 107 was one of the most multiracial schools in the city, with its student population well over two-thirds black and Latino. This was the face of one of the city's high-performing public schools. The contrast between the two scenes struck me because of what it said about the directions of housing policy, education policy, and law enforcement in Michael Bloomberg's New York, and how they contribute to maximizing segregation in the city.

Though the Bloomberg administration has constructed a significant amount of affordable housing and has made it a priority to give parents in poor neighborhoods more options through the development of charter schools, it has not made fostering integrated schools or communities a priority. The vast majority of affordable housing the city government has built has been located in already hypersegregated communities like the South Bronx, and the vast majority of charter schools it has approved have had 100 percent black and Latino populations. One result is that in the neighborhood where I have lived for the last thirty-five years, Park Slope, excellent public schools that were once a third white, a third black, and a third Latino, and with enormous income diversity, have become majority white and affluent.

The loss of educational opportunities for black, Latino, and working-class families this entailed by this evolution has been maximized by the city government's approach to market-level housing. Had the city government required that all market-level housing designate 30 to 40 percent of all units as affordable, then the proliferation of new housing developments in Park Slope would not have changed the demographic character of the neighborhood and the neighborhood schools. But because so much of affordable housing in the city has been constructed in neighborhoods where the public schools are segregated and struggling, the opportunity to create high-quality integrated public schools has been lost.

This in turn affects the "choices" the city is offering working-class parents and parents of color. Instead of giving them the option of sending their children to integrated public schools with top teachers, innovative curricula, and excellent arts program, the city offers parents only the chance to attend highly regimented, ethnically homogeneous charter schools, some of which drive out children with special needs or children who can't adapt to the schools' rigid discipline. What we have, at the extreme, is a Promise Academy for working-class blacks and a PS 107 for affluent whites; each committed to educational excellence, but following strategies for achieving that excellence that are totally contradictory to one another, and separating young people of different race and class backgrounds from each another. When you add stop and frisk to the mix, the result is an ever more segregated city. Is this the kind of environment we want our children to grow up in? It's time to start making the development of culturally and economically diverse communities the city's top priority, even if it undermines the city's character as a playground for the global rich.

FRIDAY, JUNE 29, 2012

The Battle Against Corporate School Reform Must Be Waged Locally Before It Can Succeed Nationally

For the foreseeable future, the battle to save public education from uncontrolled testing and corporate control will not be won at the national level. Both political parties are in the pockets of the billionaire reformers, and the national leadership of teachers unions are desperately trying to save their organizations by making compromises that will leave them free to fight another day. This means that teachers, students, and parents are on their own in challenging policies that dumb down the curriculum, undermine creative thinking, squeeze out the arts, and put young people's health at risk by eliminating physical activity during and after school.

Every policy being promoted nationally by each political party works to turn schools into zones of fear and stress for students and those who work in them. All across the nation, these policies are producing a simmering rage. But since that rage gets no support or recognition from elected officials, and is largely disregarded by commercial media, most people nurture their rage in private or in small group discussions among families or friends. This is where we—education activists—come in. Whether we are teachers, principals, parents, students, or just concerned citizens, we must provide leadership on the local level that affirms the validity of this rage and turns it into action.

The first step is to join the discussions about how public education is being destroyed wherever it takes place. We must do this at the workplace, in the hair salon, at Little League practice, in the doctor's office, at PTA and union meetings. Let people know that they are not alone, that there are national organizations working to help people fight back against excessive testing, to restore play, arts, and recess, and to stop the closing of schools against the wishes of the communities they are located in. Wear buttons, pass out flyers, let everyone in contact with you know where you stand. And don't worry about political affiliation. When it comes to fighting to make sure children enjoy school and are not beaten down by testing, you will find support runs the gamut from the Tea Party to revolutionary socialists.

Then start organizing local actions that are winnable, whether it involves picketing school boards to demand the restoration of sports, arts, and music, or collective actions that involve opting out or walking out of tests. Make your protests fun and sponsor dinners, picnics, and benefit concerts to promote your activities. And once you get a following, start working on local elected officials to get them to support you. You are much more likely to make headway with people who depend on parent and teacher votes to be elected than with national party officials who depend on big contributions from billionaire education reforms to fund their campaigns.

Having raised my voice about the threat to public education at every venue I have mentioned—at the salon where I get my hair cut, at my granddaughter's track practice, in my office at work, at my tennis club, and at family gatherings and parties to which I have been invited—I can assure you that a growing variety of people agree with me that excessive testing is destroying our schools. So don't give up, and don't beat your head against the wall because your governor and both major parties' presidential candidates won't listen to a word you stay. This battle has to be won one neighborhood, one school, and one city at a time. When something this wrong has been unleashed, we have to give people the confidence to follow their own best instincts. We must not only become leaders, we must try to become the heroes we spent our lives looking up to. The crisis we face demands nothing less.

MONDAY, JUNE 25, 2012

Why Business Leaders Make a Mess When They Are Put in Charge of Schools—a Personal Reflection

Every time I have a conversation with people who have been successful in business—something that happens more than you might think because of the sports I play, tennis and golf—it strikes me they have no understanding of what motivates teachers. As people who have marked their own success in life through the accumulation of income, investments, and property, they find it hard to respect people whose personal satisfaction comes largely through nonmaterial rewards. They think it odd that a person as competitive as I am on the court could devote myself to a field where I have no chance of becoming rich, and look on most teachers and professors with a bemused contempt that I only get an exemption from because of my sports skills. This is why it is frightening that business leaders have taken charge of education in the United States. The only things they take seriously as motivation are material rewards and fear of losing one's job or business, so they are convinced that schools in the United States can only be improved if a business style reward-and-punishment system is given primacy.

They love the idea of performance evaluations based on hard data, with student test scores being the equivalent of sales figures and profits, merit increments for those who succeed, and removal of those who fail. However, because they fail to understand how much of a teacher's job satisfaction comes from relationship building and watching students develop over a lifetime, they create systems of evaluation that totally eliminate such experiences because they cannot be reliably measured. The result, sad to say, is that measurement trumps real learning.

The inevitable results are massive demoralization of the teaching force (teacher morale is now at the lowest in recorded history); a narrowing of the curriculum to constant test preparation; and a "brain drain" of talented teachers from high-poverty schools to those located in more prosperous neighborhoods. Why we allowed people who are successful in one field control of a field in where they have no experience and no track record is a question historians in the future, will need to ponder, but the results, so far, have been near catastrophic.

All across the country, we have more and more teachers who hate their jobs because their job security has been destroyed, and more and more children who hate school because of the constant testing. It's time to change course. The Great Recession should have shattered once and for all the idea that the measurement and motivation systems of American business are superior to those in the public sector. For example, do we want the same quality of teacher ratings as Moody's and Standard and Poor's applied to mortgage-based derivatives? American business needs to clean up its own act, and not apply its flawed methods to other fields. If we continue on the path we are on, we may well see the American education system become as corrupt and unstable as the global financial system.

TUESDAY, MAY 29, 2012

What Is Lost When Teaching as a Lifetime Calling Is Undermined: A Personal Reflection

Today teachers in elementary schools through the universities are the targets of a ferocious effort to force them to conform to private sector norms of accountability, productivity, and market-driven competition. The assault takes two major forms: an effort to quantify student learning so that teacher effectiveness can be easily judged, and an effort to weaken or eliminate teacher tenure so that teachers can be removed, or rewarded, based on their effectiveness. The goal of these reforms is to have teachers work under conditions that more closely resemble those of workers in the private sector, and to place them under fierce and continuous pressure to improve their productivity.

The underlying assumption is that our educational system is expensive and undermines the competitiveness of the American economy in the global marketplace. This argument, I have discovered, has an irresistible appeal to those who have spent their lives in the private sector, especially those who have risen to the top through what they believe are their own talents and abilities. They see teacher tenure as a luxury society can no longer afford, as it rewards inefficiency and retards innovation.

Their views have found an echo in the policies of both major parties so teachers, at all levels, will have to justify themselves on the basis of regular performance assessments dictated by federal and state governments, rather than teachers' professional associations. Most teachers, especially the most talented and committed ones, view these reforms with horror. Not only are they extremely skeptical of the private sector's vaunted "efficiency," a legitimate concern given the astronomical compensation private companies give their executives, they fear that the way classroom learning will be assessed erases those aspects of classroom teaching that make it life-changing for student and teacher, and in the process, teaching will be turned into a revolving door profession. This is not an idle concern. Every teaching evaluation, instrument I know treats the individual class as a self-contained entity and tries to measure or assess what learning took place only during the time that class met. But the best teachers I know don't just try to promote mastery of a fixed body of material, they try to impart ways of thinking, and ways of seeing the world, that will influence their students long after they leave any particular class.

They also promote that dimension of "lifetime learning." They remain in touch with their students long after they leave their classes, and even draw upon former students to help teach current ones. These lifelong connections are among the most important things that keep great teachers in the classroom, yet I have never seen a policy maker so much as mention them in proposals for how to improve American schools. I know this all sounds very abstract, even self-serving, to people who have not been teachers so I want to give a few examples from my own experience.

I have been teaching nearly forty-five years, starting first with high school students in the Columbia Upward Bound Program, then moving on to undergraduates and graduate students at Fordham University. Both of my parents were lifetime educators in the New York City public schools so I had models of professionalism and dedication to draw upon. But I also brought my own political experiences, my research on black history and passion for racial justice into the classroom, and viewed my students as people I was trying to empower, as well as to teach. Because of the subject matter I was teaching, African American history, and the time I was teaching it, the late '60s and early '70s, there was no scripted curriculum for what I was doing. I invented my courses as I went along with the help other young scholars in the field, and gave my students great freedom to interpret the material.

My courses incorporated room for debates and performances, used music as a guide to historical understanding, and produced class publications. I also spent time with my students outside of class, playing ball with them, attending cultural events and demonstrations, and meeting them for one-on-one tutoring sessions when necessary. The result was that I developed connections with some of my students that lasted a lifetime. How these connections helped my students I can only speculate, but they had a tremendous effect on my own effectiveness as a scholar and teacher.

One of the first students I ever taught in the Columbia Upward Bound Program, William Wright, had as great an influence on my life as any professor I had in college. William was on the board of governors of the Institute of Afro-American Studies at Fordham as a student representative when I was hired as a faculty member in 1970. Even though I was may have been the first white faculty member ever hired by a black studies program, this department has remained my home for the last forty-two years, and a great home it has been. But that wasn't all. When my book *White Boy: A Memoir* came out in 2002, William, who was then news director of BET, commis-

sioned a three-minute special on it, which led to numerous speaking opportunities at universities and broadcast media. But most importantly,
William's daughter, Patricia Wright, undergraduate and then a graduate
student at Fordham, became the first graduate assistant of the research
project I founded, the Bronx African American History Project (BAAHP),
and was instrumental in organizing a huge benefit concert featuring the
Bronx's greatest doo-wop singers which attracted more than seven hundred
people, and put the BAAHP on the map—locally and nationally—as an innovative community history project. But there's more.

Two of the first students I taught at Fordham in fall 1970 and 1971,
and whom I got to know as fellow activists in the Fordham antiwar movement, Kathy Palmer and Sally Dunford, are still active in the Bronx. Kathy
is a teacher at a local elementary school, and Sally as a housing organizer
and community advocate. When I was supervising senior theses this year,
each proved instrumental in advising my students on the issues they were
investigating. And this was not the first time I called on them as advisors
on student projects, or for help with my research. Kathy has been enor-
mously helpful in setting up interviews for the Bronx African American
History Project, and Sally has spoken in my classes and employed students
as interns in her housing group.

Finally, the BAAHP, which is now one of the premier community-based
oral history projects in the nation, has grown and flourished because of the
generosity of two groups—Bronx residents past and present—who want
to see their stories told and stereotypes about the Bronx defused. Furthermore, former students in our department who are proud to see the lessons
they learned incorporated into a groundbreaking research initiative. Without
the individual contributions of our students—some who go back to the
1970s and some who graduated only a year or two ago—the BAAHP, which
now has conducted over three hundred oral history interviews, could not
exist in its current form. We are not talking about a small number of people.
At least a hundred former students are regular BAAHP supporters, a remarkable total for a department as small as ours, and a tribute to the way
our department faculty have approached teaching as a mission, not just a
job, while building relationships with students that have lasted a lifetime. I
share these stories to explain how my former students have enhanced my

life personally and professionally, and affirm the value of honoring teaching as a lifelong profession. Teachers must have the autonomy to decide what takes place in their classrooms, be able to view classroom learning through the lens of relationship building and skill instruction.

Current reforms, if taken to their logical conclusions, will undermine all those goals and make our schools places where inquiry and imagination are stifled. Students and teachers will always be looking over their shoulders to see if they have violated some rule. If that happens, something very precious in our lives will have been lost.

Education Reformers and the "New Jim Crow"

If somebody told me fifteen years ago, when I was spending many of my days working with community groups in the Bronx and East New York dealing with the consequences of the crack epidemic, that you could solve the problems of neighborhoods under siege by insulating students in local schools from the conditions surrounding them and by devoting every ounce of teachers' energies to raising their test scores, I would have said, "What planet are you living on?" Students were bringing the stresses of their daily lives into the classroom in ways that no teacher with a heart could ignore, and these stresses created obstacles to concentrating in school, much less completing homework. People living in middle-class communities couldn't imagine these forces. To be effective in getting students to learn, teachers had to be social workers, surrogate parents, and neighborhood protectors, as well as people imparting skills. At times, the interpersonal dimensions of their work were more important than the strictly instructional components.

The leaders of the education reform movement, from Secretary Arne Duncan—to the head of Teach for America, to Michelle Rhee, to the heads of almost every urban school system—regard discussions of neighborhood conditions as impediments to the quest to achieve educational equity, and demand that teachers shut out the conditions they are living in. Teachers must now inspire, prod, and discipline their charges to achieve results on standardized tests that match those of their middle-class counterparts living in more favorable conditions.

The position they are taking, that schools in depressed areas can be radically improved without doing anything to improve conditions in the neighborhoods they are located in, flies in the face of the common sense of anyone who lives or works in such communities, so much so that it represents a form of collective madness! The idea that an entire urban school system (not a few favored schools) can be uplifted strictly through school-based reforms, such as eliminating teacher tenure or replacing public schools with charter schools, without changing *any* of the conditions driving people further into poverty is contrary to anyone's lived experience and has in fact, never been accomplished anywhere in the world. Let me break down for you what the "no excuses" approach to school reform means in commonsense terms.

Basically, reformers propose to raise test scores and radically improve graduation rates in urban school systems without doing anything to:

1. Reduce homelessness, residential instability, and housing overcrowding as factors in student's lives.
2. Deal with hunger, poor diet, and obesity as factors impeding education performance.
3. Challenge racial profiling and police violence in student's lives, not only in their neighborhoods, but in the schools.
4. Deal with unemployment, underemployment, and wage compression as factors in the lives of students and their families.
5. Deal with the impact of the prison industrial complex on students and their families, particularly the psychic and economic stress of having close relatives in prison, and having them be unemployable when they return.
6. Deal with the trauma of domestic violence and peer violence as it impacts students' lives and their educational performance.
7. Deal with the way students are profiled by police, store owners, and ordinary citizens when they leave their neighborhoods and go into downtown business districts or middle-class neighborhoods.

Essentially, reformers are asking everyone involved with schools in underresourced communities, especially teachers and administrators, to block out all the conditions that Michelle Alexander has highlighted in her book *The New Jim Crow*. Not only will this approach fail miserably, it gives a free pass to economic and political elites who policies helped create the very conditions that lock people into poverty.

No wonder billionaires love these policies. It takes the onus off of them for concentrating so much of the nation's wealth in the top 1 percent of the population. No wonder politicians love it. It absolves them of responsibility for building the largest prison system in the industrialized world, filling it with poor people and people of color, and creating huge police forces and drug enforcement policies that assure such prisons are filled.

Essentially, current school reform policies represent a brilliant tactic to avoid dealing with the real causes of poverty and inequality in society, while finding a convenient scapegoat in public school teachers and their unions. These policies are transparent, ill considered, and immoral. And over time, people in the communities most targeted by these reforms will rise up in protest.

THURSDAY, APRIL 5, 2012

Disparate Impact Gone Awry: How the Misapplication of Civil Rights Law Encouraged the Demonization of the Nation's Teachers

One of the unexamined dimensions of the history of the school reform movement is the role that civil rights lawyers have played in shaping its guiding assumptions and strategies. I was reminded of this the other day when reading an unpublished manuscript by an Oklahoma City–based teacher named John Thompson. Thompson pointed out that civil rights lawyers typically demonstrated the existence of discrimination by documenting statistical disparities between underrepresented and privileged groups, which is precisely the approach school reformers used in devising remedies for the achievement, or test score, gap between black and white students. Reformers looked at statistical disparities between schools in black and white neighborhoods, and inferred that the lower test scores and graduation rates in the former could best be remedied by removing teachers and administrators in the underperforming institutions, replacing them with more skilled people, closing such schools, and replacing them with new schools with greater flexibility in hiring.

As I read these passages, they struck a chord on multiple levels. First, I thought of my own research on the evolution of affirmative action, and how civil rights leaders and federal officials developed a rationale for it. Affirmative action began when policy makers required employers to do statistical analyses of the percentage of underrepresented groups they hired or enrolled, and based remedial action on those statistics rather than demonstrated discriminatory intent. The main agency responsible for enforcing antidiscrimination law in employment, the Equal Employment Opportunity Commission (EEOC), pioneered this approach. When companies complained that underrepresentation of minorities was not the result of intentional discrimination, their complaints were rejected by the EEOC and the federal courts, which invoked a doctrine called "disparate impact" (enshrined in a Supreme Court decision *Griggs v. Duke Power*. This doctrine stipulated that practices that reinforced historic patterns of discrimination, even when they were neutral in intent and application, were considered discriminatory under federal law. These practices could be subject to remedies that increased the number of employees from the group in question, even if the institution's normal standards for hiring were set aside.

Now, let's move ahead forty years. Civil rights lawyers began looking at disparities in achievement between black and white students through a similar lens, treating such disparities as if they were the product of discrimination. But rather than viewing those disparities as the result of discrimination in criminal justice policy, the housing and employment markets, and access to family wealth, they chose to isolate the school from the depressed neighborhood they were located in, and put continuous pressure on underperforming schools to do better jobs educating black and Latino students.

One incidental outcome of the application of disparate impact theory to education was the identification of "bad teachers," and the unions that protect them, as the primary causes of discriminatory outcomes for black and Latino students. These were factors that policy makers felt they could directly influence, unlike intergenerational poverty and discrimination in housing, employment, and criminal justice. And once the schools became isolated from their neighborhood setting as discriminatory institutions, teachers quickly became the main targets of remedial action.

But demonizing teachers was not the only consequence of this style of thinking. Once policy makers began developing statistical models to reliably compare and rate schools, and gauge teacher and administrator performance, they realized that they needed a much more reliable data base upon which to do this. This meant increasing the number of standardized tests, applying them across the board to constituencies that had previously been exempted—such as ELL and special needs students—and spending huge amounts of money on software to process the information and consultants to analyze that information.

The demonization of teachers and the proliferation of testing, took place in New York City under the direction of well-known civil rights attorney James Leibman, from the faculty of Columbia Law School, who was hired by Chancellor Joel Klein, another lawyer who loved to employ civil rights rhetoric as the Department of Education's first accountability officer. Under Leibman's direction, the DOE created complex statistical models first to grade schools, and later to evaluate teacher performance, each using criteria that based ratings on complex measures involving variations in student test scores from year to year. On the basis of the models, which were statistically flawed and often defied common sense, schools were closed and teachers were removed and placed in a much-stigmatized reserve pool. The consequence was an increase in the number of tests, and huge ratcheting-up of stress levels associated with them. In New York City, for example, every third grader must sit through six straight days of testing for ninety minutes a day. Those who defend this practice still use the language of equity in explaining why they are doing this. But quite frankly, the negatives associated with this level of quantification are far exceeding the benefits.

We now face a situation where school reform policies once described as necessary to achieve educational equity and reduce the racial achievement gap have resulted in uncontrolled testing; profit taking on a grand scale by test companies; and attacks on teacher integrity and collective bargaining rights that have produced the lowest levels of teacher morale on record.

Such is the consequence of the misapplication of a once honorable civil rights doctrine to a setting in which the most publicized causes of discrimination—teacher apathy and incompetence—are far less significant than environmental factors excluded from the analytical and statistical model, particularly poverty and societal racism.

The notion that "school reform is the civil rights cause of the twenty-first century" has become a cruel joke to teachers and students who find themselves deluged with unnecessary tests, and placed under intolerable stress in the name of educational equity.

FRIDAY, MARCH 30, 2012

Schools Played Little Role in America's Most Dramatic Phase of Wealth Equalization and Are Unlikely to Play a Meaningful Role Now

At a time when inequalities in wealth are greater than they have been at any time since the late 1920s, leaders in both parties are looking to changes in public education as major vehicles for achieving greater opportunity and equity in our economic system. Unfortunately, there is no historical evidence that schools have ever played that role. Take a close look at the chart in Paul Krugman's column ("The Conscience of a Liberal," *New York Times*, September 18, 2007). The most dramatic redistribution of wealth in American history took place in the years 1937 to 1947, when the percentage of income accruing to the top 10 percent of earners plummeted to half its previous total, and remained there for over thirty years. Not surprisingly, those were also the years when black per capita income grew fastest relative to white per capita income (from 44 percent in 1940 to 57 percent in 1950).

What was responsible for this redistribution of income? Was it increased investment in education or reform in the nations public schools? As it turns out, the major factors were increased taxation on high incomes; a substantial growth in the percentage of workers covered by union contracts (from less than five million in 1937 to ore than fifteen million in 1945); a reduction in racial discrimination in basic industry (due to the Fair Employment Practices Commission); and rapid rural-to-urban migration, as a result of wartime economic recovery. These policies led to a dramatically transformed and increasingly multiracial industrial working class that was highly organized and politically influential at the local and national levels, and capable of defending its interests relative to large corporations and the wealthy far greater than its counterparts twenty years earlier.

Now, let's segue back to today. The idea that school reform strategies emphasizing testing, accountability, privatization, and limiting teacher union power will somehow result in greater economic and racial equality has become an article of faith in the Democratic and Republican parties, and has been embraced by the Obama administration. But there is absolutely no evidence that it is working. Every social indicator of educational achievement, employment, and wealth distribution suggests that our nation is *more* unequal now that it was when No Child Left Behind was passed (2001), and no improvements have been made since the introduction of Race to the Top (2009). If these reforms aren't working now, and have never worked in the past, why do many people believe they are effective?

Some of this reflects the power of foundations funded by the nation's wealthiest people (Walton, Gates, Broad, and so on) in promoting school reform ideology, but it also reflects the discomfort of much of the American population with collectivist solutions to social problems even when they work.

The truth is we can do a lot more to promote racial and economic equality through programs of progressive taxation, promotion of unionization in low-wage enterprises, and efforts to uproot discrimination in the labor market and the criminal justice system than by trying to improve our public schools through competition and privatization. But those measures require sacrifices by the very wealthy that school reform avoids, so it will take fierce grassroots pressure to bring them to fruition.

FRIDAY, MARCH 16, 2012

Squeezing the Life out of Children: The Deadly Impact of Testing Protocols Derived from No Child Left Behind and Race to the Top

When I first started work on this "Educators Letter to President Obama" early in January, my first thought was focused on all the teachers being demoralized by a campaign of demonization orchestrated from Washington that aimed to hold them accountable for student performance on standardized tests. I feared that the best teachers would be driven out of our schools, and that teaching would become a stress-filled, temporary profession, and public school systems viewed as sources of profit by the nation's most powerful corporations. None of those initial fears have receded, but they have been increasingly supplemented by another concern—that the strategies developed to rate teachers, which involve the proliferation of high-stakes tests beginning in the lowest grades—are squeezing the life out of students, and making them hate school.

This is not a concern I have made up based on secondhand information. It reflects conversations, some solicited, some overheard, with and among parents of elementary school students who cannot believe how learning expectations have been ratcheted up at the expense of play and class projects. "My son is seven years old. How can they expect him to sit at his desk for six hours a day writing things down?" one mother at my granddaughter's track practice said yesterday. "Just wait," another mother said. "In third grade, they will have six days in a row of tests for ninety minutes a day. My son is a nervous wreck." A few people I know have responded to this atmosphere by homeschooling their children, but as these friends pointed out to me, this is not a realistic option for most working-class parents.

Are these people and their children doomed to ten years of torture introduced in the name of "restoring national competitiveness," "preparing young people for the job market," and "weeding out bad teachers"?

They are unless you do something about it. Signing and circulating this petition (at dumpduncan.org) is one way of sending a message that excessive testing is demoralizing our children and undermining the teaching profession, and that Washington needs to start listening to teachers, parents, and students themselves.

THURSDAY, FEBRUARY 23, 2012

"Goodbye, Kotter": The Transformation of the Image of the Inner-City Teacher in American Popular Culture

When I was driving to work today, I was thinking how strange it is that the inner-city teacher has become the subject of a discourse of demonization in almost every portion of American society, from Hollywood, to the press, to business and foundation leadership, to the White House and the US Department of Education. The defining moment for me, in terms of seeing the teacher as scapegoat for the nation's problems, was when the secretary of education and the president praised the mass firing of teachers in Central Falls, Rhode Island, but the barrage has continued with the production of the movie *Waiting for Superman*, the Hollywood film *Bad Teacher*, and the recent vicious attacks on teachers and teachers unions by New York City mayor Michael Bloomberg, New York governor Andrew Cuomo, and New Jersey governor Chris Christie. If you followed this argument, you would think that "bad teachers" and their defenders were responsible for the persistence of poverty, the black-white test score gap, and the weakness of the United States in the global economy.

It was not always thus. While teachers have always been a subject of bemused contempt, with expressions like "those who can do, those who can't teach" being part of the national vocabulary, it is also true that there were once many powerful images of the inner-city teacher/principal/coach as hero in American popular culture. From *Up the Down Staircase* to *Dangerous Minds* to *Stand and Deliver*, Hollywood gave us portraits of teachers who devoted their lives to helping students in tough circumstances gain confidence and realize their potential. These positive portrayals also extended to sports and the arts, where three of my all-time favorite movies showed the power of teachers who worked in those areas to work miracles—*Fame*, *Wildcats*, and *Remember the Titans*. And finally, in the world of television sitcoms, there was *Welcome Back, Kotter*, which presented a humorous but ultimately inspirational picture of a person who returned to teach in the Brooklyn high school he attended.

I feel a deep sense of sadness in writing this. There are still heroes teaching and serving as principals in some of the nation's toughest neighborhoods. I know scores of such individuals in the Bronx—one of whom, Principal Paul Cannon of PS 140 in the Morrisania section of the Bronx, has become a dear friend. Yet popular discourse about education erases their accomplishments in inspiring and motivating students in favor of a narrow obsession with test scores.

How can we inspire young people devote their lives to the teaching profession if 90 percent of what we say about teachers is disparaging or contemptuous?

The answer, of course, is that we can't and we won't. If we stay on the current path, teaching will become a temporary job, teachers who have little emotional stake in their jobs and who view them in strictly instrumental terms—as takers of tests determine whose results teachers' professional status. If we were to produce a sitcom today, we would have to call it *Goodbye, Kotter* because the real teachers, the ones who love their students and see their careers as a lifetime calling, are being driven out.

When the "Best and the Brightest" Don't Have the Answers: President Obama's Flawed Approach to School Reform

When Barack Obama ascended to the presidency he was fired up with a desire to improve America's schools, which he felt were falling behind those in other advanced countries. He decided to bring "the best minds in the country" in to help them with this task—CEOs of successful businesses, heads of major foundations, young executives from management consulting firms—to figure out a strategy to transform America's schools, especially those in low-performing districts. He promised them full support of his administration when they finally came up with effective strategies, including the use of federal funding to persuade, and if necessary, compel local districts to implement them.

Notably missing in this brain trust were representatives of America's teachers and school administrators, but their absence was not accidental. Because the president and his chief education adviser Arne Duncan believed that a key problem in America's schools was the low quality of the people working in them, they felt no need to include principals and teachers in the administration's education planning, especially since those plans involved putting pressure on them to perform, and then removing those who couldn't meet the new standards.

From a management standpoint the reforms developed, which included promoting competition, universalizing teacher evaluation based on student test scores, and introducing merit pay, made perfect sense. However, since none of the people developing the reforms had spent much time in a classroom or were willing to spend a significant part of their lives performing the jobs they were reshaping, they had little idea what their reforms meant "on the ground." They had even less evidence that these reforms would be effective when implemented.

Now three years later, after all these new policies have been put into effect in New York, Chicago, Philadelphia, and Buffalo, there is no evidence that America's schools are performing better than when the president entered office, or that the test score gap between wealthy and poor districts is decreasing. But evidence and experience doesn't seem to matter when you bring "the best minds in the country" together to develop a strategy. Come on, how can Bill Gates, Eli Broad, Michael Bloomberg, and the Ivy League gurus from Teach for America be wrong, and graduates of state teachers colleges and teacher education programs be right?

But reality has a way of intruding even on "the best and the brightest" when the fundamental assumptions that guide policy are wrong. This happened during the war in Vietnam, when an indigenous nationalist revolution was treated as an arm of a global Communist conspiracy. It is happening now when school failures due to poverty and inequality are being blamed on incompetent teachers and administrators.

So as in Vietnam, we will invest hundreds of billions, maybe trillions of dollars in a cause, which, at the end of the day, will turn into a fool's errand and undermine the careers and demean the efforts of the nation's teachers, dividing communities against themselves, while fattening the pockets of consulting firms, test companies, and online learning entrepreneurs.

And ten years down the road, when all the damage is done, policy makers will wake up and call America's teachers back in to ask, "What do you think we should do?" They will say that teaching has to be a lifetime calling, and that when dealing with children, there are no miracles—opening minds, and changing lives, requires hard work, persistence, imagination, and a love for the young people you are working with. These are tasks that cannot be performed by computers or "managed" by people who have never worked with children themselves.

If You Want to Know the Human Impact of the Current Recession, Ask America's Teachers

One of the things I've discovered in recent years is that when it comes to education policy, the last people asked for input are America's teachers. We have a president who holds an" education summit" that includes the nation's top business leaders and foundation heads but no teachers; we have billionaires lobbying to privatize education and break teachers unions; we have an organization that purports to work for educational equity that encourages its recruits to leave teaching after two years because they can influence policy more by moving into other, more prestigious, careers, rather than spending a lifetime as a "mere teacher."

The results are plain to see. After ten years of No Child Left Behind, three years of Race to the Top, and twenty years of Teach for America, we have seen no change in the global standing of America's schools and no reduction in the test-score gap between racially and economically disadvantaged groups and the rest of the population.

But we lose something more than an opportunity to improve our schools by excluding teachers' voices. We lose a chance to understand the human impact of poverty and economic distress, not only those locked in intergenerational poverty, but those made newly poor by the economic crisis. Students bring the wounds of poverty into their classrooms every day, in ways that break teachers' hearts, keep them up at night, and make the accountability protocols based on test scores that "education reformers" are now imposing seem totally divorced from reality.

As someone who is married to an elementary school principal and talks to teachers almost daily because of my work in Bronx schools and my contact with former students who have chosen to teach, I have, even secondhand, been haunted by what this recession is doing to young people and their families.

One thing that leaps out at me from the teacher's stories I hear is how many students in poor and working-class neighborhoods have no secure place to stay. Students move from apartment to apartment or house to house when their parents or grandparents can't pay rent; experience bouts of homelessness and must sleep in shelters, temporary residences, and occasionally subways or cars; and move in an out of foster care. Sometimes students disappear for days or weeks at a time, sometimes they disappear altogether. But even those who come in somewhat regularly often fall asleep in class because the places they are staying are so crowded or noisy that it is difficult to sleep. I have heard these stories from teachers in inner-city schools in New York, Buffalo, and Philadelphia, but I have also heard them from teachers in suburban communities where people are sinking into poverty. Those who think the housing and foreclosure crisis in America has no impact on education need to talk to teachers, but we won't do that if we believe that low attention spans in school are largely the result of " bad teachers" protected by "evil unions."

That's one portion of the stories teachers tell. The other relates to the lack of food and medical care students in poor communities get, and how this affects their concentration levels and general well being. I will never forget how a principal and two teachers at a school located in the most decayed and dangerous housing project in the Bronx closed the door on my Sudanese colleague and I after taking us on an upbeat tour of several classes and said, "Let us tell you what is really going on here. Every Friday," the principal continued, "students in the school start crying because they afraid they may have little or nothing to eat all weekend. The only time they know they are going to have three meals a day is on school days. And because they closed down the health clinic in the project, students bring their whole families to see the school nurse. This is place that God forgot." My Sudanese colleague, by the time the principal had finished, started crying and said, "This is like a refugee camp in Africa." You think that this is the only place in the country where this kind of story could be told? Think again. Hunger and lack of medical care is a huge and growing problem among America's school children, and has a tremendous affect on their academic performance.

Then there is the growing level of violence and stress that young people experience in homes and communities where people are losing jobs, losing homes, and losing hope—violence that they bring into the school environment. I have been hearing more and more stories from teachers of kids exploding in rage, at one another and at teachers—sometimes individually, sometimes in large groups. Bedlam in hallways and classrooms is increasingly common, often set off by the minutest provocation. Some of this disorder can be attributed to chaotic school environments, but some of it stems from the extraordinary stress that students are under when they are out of school be toxic mixture of food insecurity, unstable living situations, and violence inflicted on them by people in their own households or by neighborhood gangs and crews.

None of what I am describing is new. You could have heard similar stories from teachers in poor and working-class neighborhoods in the '70s, '80s, and '90s. What is new is the extent of the suffering as more and more families whose lives were once stable get pushed into poverty.

All throughout the nation, in small towns and suburbs, in once middle-class communities as well as inner-city neighborhoods, teachers are ready to tell these stories. Will we listen or will we continue to put our heads in the sand, and blame the messengers for the message?

FRIDAY, JANUARY 13, 2012

Déjà vu All Over Again: What Happened to Industrial Workers in the '80s and '90s Is Happening to Teachers and Government Workers Today

In preparation for my course "The Worker in American Life," I am reading about the broad-based assault on industrial labor that took place during the '80s and '90s in a broad swath of the United States from New England through the Pacific Northwest. Plant closings, transfer of family businesses to international conglomerates, union busting, and finally, the destruction of a wage scale and union rules that allowed factory workers to live in comfort and security and have dignity on the job, hit the nation with the force of a juggernaut.

In industrial cities and in small towns that depended on industrial production, the results were devastating. Drug epidemics, domestic violence, gang activity, foreclosures, evictions, arson, and the erosion of once-proud business districts beset them. Some of the communities where this drama played out eventually achieved a precarious stability, but the prosperity of the postwar years never returned. Wage levels had lowered to the point where a person had to work two, possibly three, jobs to achieve the income a unionized factory worker once made, or turn to illegal activity to supplement legal income.

Now, an equally comprehensive effort to undermine workers' bargaining rights, dignity, and standard of living is under way in the country. On state and local levels, it is being led by Republican politicians who are systematically trying to strip away collective bargaining rights of government workers, and pass "right to work" laws that make union shops illegal. Initiatives of the first kind have succeeded in states that were sites of landmark labor conflicts and strong unions, Wisconsin and Ohio, and the second initiative is on the verge of being voted into law in Indiana.

It would be comforting to think that this attack on public workers is coming only from the Republican Party and the political Right, but one of the most powerful and insidious efforts to undermine public worker unionism—the attack on teachers unions—has been driven by foundations and funding sources traditionally associated with the Democratic Party and has been enthusiastically endorsed by the Obama administration. Not only did the president and his secretary of education Arne Duncan praise the firing of union teachers in Central Falls, Rhode Island, who refused to accept the unilateral revision of union rules by the local superintendent. They have provided huge financial incentives to states and municipalities to create privately managed, non-union charter schools, and also adopt procedures for rating teachers based on student test scores so teachers judged "incompetent" by these criteria may be fired.

Make no mistake about it, the sum effect of these initiatives, if successful, will be strikingly similar to the offensive against industrial unions in the '80s and '90s—it will drive down wage levels substantially, and erode dignity on the job for those subject to new managerial prerogatives.

How this will help the communities in which this large group of workers lose income, self-respect, and in some cases, employment, is hard to imagine.

It will hurt families, businesses, the housing market, and in all probability, lower wage levels in the private sector as a new source of surplus labor is created. What benefits accrue in lower taxes will hardly compensate for the losses.

If you don't believe me, just visit Buffalo, New York, Youngstown, Ohio, or Johnstown, Pennsylvania and other once-thriving cities where high worker incomes and job security produced thriving neighborhoods of working-class homeowners. Now there are huge stretches in each city where every other lot is vacant; where business district feature groceries, liquor stores, and storefront churches; and where the drug business is the major source of income for a significant group of young men and growing number of young women.

Let me put the matter bluntly. The last wave of union-busting left physical and moral damage that we have not fully recovered from. The new wave about to descend on us will add to the destruction, and perhaps push the social fabric to the breaking point.

There is a phrase "a rising tide lifts all boats." Unfortunately, the reverse is true as well. If we stand by and not defend teachers and other government workers as their unions are broken, their dignity undermined, and their wage levels shattered by powerful interests who profit from their distress, we will accelerate the transformation of the United States into a plutocracy where the majority of people are living on the edge of poverty, a small elite controls all levels of government, and parlays that into unimaginable benefits for themselves.

This is the future that awaits us. Which side are you on?

Wednesday, January 9, 2013

My Vision for Revitalizing Public Education

I have a very different vision of what public schools should be doing than Bill Gates, Michelle Rhee, Jeb Bush, Arne Duncan, Michael Bloomberg, and the current generation of "school reformers" does.

My vision involves making schools centers of community revitalization where young people's curiosity and creativity is nurtured; where student differences are recognized and respected; where the physical and emotional health of children is promoted; where teachers have long careers; and where parents and community members are welcome.

I think you begin with creating a child-friendly environment. That means sharply reducing the number of tests; leaving ample room for exercise and play; giving primacy to the arts; and having instruction in subject areas that when possible incorporate hands-on learning and project-based activity.

I would also like as many schools as possible to grow and prepare food (with indoor and outdoor farms) and link that to science instruction; have students participate in community improvement initiatives; have students use computers they can carry with them rather than forcing them to use them at desks; and have students become involved in mentoring younger students.

As much as possible, I would like learning to be cooperative rather than competitive, and extend that to the teaching staff. This would mean removing the threat of school closings, and having evaluation done by peers using multiple measures, rather than by consultants deriving their data from student test scores.

I would also like to see an end to the "one path fits all" approach to secondary education, and revive the vocational and technical schools that were once fixtures in our educational mix to prepare students for decent-paying jobs in traditional trades such as automobile and appliance repair, as well as emerging areas like solar and wind energy and environmental friendly agriculture. Here, we can learn a great deal from how Germany and other Northern European countries have done this.

Additionally, I would try to create a climate where talented people enter teaching as a lifetime career, which involves treating teachers with respec; giving them input into all decisions affecting their professional lives, including those made at the city, state, and national level; and ending attacks on their collective bargaining rights.

Right now, the basic thrust of education policy is making teachers hate teaching, students dread going to school, and parents fear that their children's love of learning will be snuffed out by excessive testing. We can do better, but only if our basic goals are to make schools places where young people are inspired and nurtured, and where teaching is treated as a lifetime calling that allows talented people the opportunity to work collaboratively and creatively.

MONDAY, JANUARY 7, 2013

Is Diane Ravitch the George Ball of Our Generation, and Education Reform Our Vietnam?

In the spring and summer of 1965, as US policy makers debated whether to send large numbers of US ground troops to Vietnam to ensure that the South Vietnamese government would not collapse, a longtime Washington insider named George Ball issued a fierce warning that the policy being recommended would be disastrous. Declaring that the conflict in Vietnam was a "civil war among Asians" not a front of a global struggle against Communism, Ball warned that sending US ground troops would lead to national humiliation no matter how large the force sent, or the technological advantage it possessed, because it would cement the character of the war on the Vietnamese side as a struggle against a foreign invader. Ball's advice, needless to say, was disregarded, and the result was exactly as he predicted—a humiliating defeat for the US that extracted a terrifying toll in deaths, and ecological damage on the Vietnamese people.

Though less immediately destructive, the bipartisan movement to revitalize public education in the United States and eliminate racial and economic gaps in educational performance has prompted an equally momentous dissent from a Washington insider, education scholar Dr. Diane Ravitch. An undersecretary of education in the George H. W. Bush administration and an initial supporter of the landmark No Child Left Behind legislation, Ravitch became convinced that the fundamental assumption that undergirded the bipartisan education reform—that the "achievement gap" between black and Latino and white and Asian students was caused by "bad teachers" and recalcitrant teachers unions rather than entrenched poverty—would lead to policy recommendations that would demoralize teachers, destabilize the nation's public school system, encourage privatization and profiteering, and increase performance gaps between racial and economic groups.

As with George Ball before her, Dr. Ravitch's recommendations were systematically ignored not only by the administration that appointed her, but the administration that replaced it. And as with George Ball, her warnings are proving to be eerily prophetic. All over the nation, policies are being implemented that are leading to demoralization of teachers; to closing of schools that honorably served communities for generations; to marginalization of special needs and ELL students; to testing scandals in high-needs schools and districts; and to an uncontrolled proliferation of tests that has put profits in the pockets of test companies, and pushed aside science, history, and the arts while making a growing number of students hate going to school.

The question is not whether these policies—an odd mixture of privatization, universal testing, and teacher/school accountability based on student test scores—will be effective in reducing the impact of poverty on educational performance. The question is how much damage will be done before a critical portion of the public, the media, and the nation's political leadership realizes how counterproductive these policies are.

If the war in Vietnam is any precedent, such a "national wake up call" on educational policy could be quite long in coming, and the damage inflicted immense. And as with that awful war, only massive protest and civil disobedience will be able to stop the policy in its tracks.

MONDAY, MARCH 18, 2013
Education Quiz for the Day

School reformers are:
1. Sincere idealists who have desperately, albeit mistakenly, seized on transforming schools as our one and only chance to make

headway against rapidly growing poverty and inequality.

2. Opportunists who have seen which way the wind is blowing, and have decided to build careers on implementing the reform agenda of testing and privatization (especially school chancellors, charter school administrators, and professors of education).

3. Politicians and media commentators who have decided that school reform is the wave of the future because the wealthiest and most powerful people in the country all support it.

3. Billionaires who spend so much money pushing the reform program that it disguises the fact that the measures they endorse are unsupported by research and are in fact batshit crazy.

4. All of the above.

WEDNESDAY, MARCH 27, 2013
What Real "School Choice" Would Look Like

It is amazing to me to see so many school reformers talk about "choice" when most teachers, students, and parents experience their policies as raw coercion. The best example of this is testing. States like New York are not only imposing large numbers of new tests to ensure compliance with the Common Core Standards and ensure that teachers can be evaluated on the basis of student test scores, they are withholding funds from school districts that refuse to use tests for teacher evaluations and telling parents that it is illegal to opt their children out of state tests.

That is choice? Sounds more like regimentation and intimidation to me—a one-size-fits-all standard for all school districts, schools, and families in the entire state. I have a better plan. Here is what New York State could do to ensure real school choice and offer many different models of how schools can function.

1. Allow any parent to withhold their child from state testing without penalty to the family, the school, or the school district. Parents should have the right to decide whether state tests are developmentally appropriate for their own child.

2.   Allow and even encourage school districts to create more "portfolio schools," like New York City's wonderful Urban Academy, which have exemption from state tests and use other measures of student achievement.

3.   Allow local school districts, rather than the state, to decide whether they want to use test scores as a component of teacher evaluations. Leave that to elected school boards, not the governor, the legislature, or the state education commissioner to decide.

These three simple "reforms" would do much to counteract the feeling, held by many, many teachers, parents, and school board members that they are living in a dictatorship where their views have no weight. They would encourage a burst of creativity as new kinds of schools are created along more democratic principles, and restore enthusiasm among teaching staffs whose morale has been broken by top-down policies based on mistrust of their professional expertise, and contempt for their input.

The only people who would lose would be test companies who see their profits go down. It's time to change direction.

MONDAY, APRIL 22, 2013

Has the War on Teachers Morphed into a War on Children?

When I first got involved in education activism four years ago, with the publication of the piece "In Defense of Public School Teachers," I did so because the elected officials in New York and around the nation were blaming public school teachers for problems in the society that were not of their making, and trying to subject them to numbers-based "accountability" protocols that would squeeze the life out of teaching under the mantle of "school reform." I saw the best teachers I knew, those who were my former students, and those I worked with in Bronx community history projects, increasingly demonized and marginalized by people who had little real-life understanding of what their jobs entailed. Since they lacked the power to speak freely about what was happening to them, I felt it was my duty to speak on their behalf.

Four years later, there is still just as much pain and rage among the nation's teachers. Now that I am publicly identified as a "teachers advocate," I probably get four or five emails or Facebook messages a week from teachers around the nation describing the fear, stress, humiliation, and erosion of professional autonomy they are experiencing as student test scores have become the major indicator of judging teacher effectiveness. It is because of such experiences that I have launched, with the support of United Opt Out, a Teachers Oral History Project that will allow teachers' viewpoints on current education policies to be recorded and preserved.

But this past week, as I have become involved with an opt-out movement in New York State that has inspired thousands of families to demand that their children be allowed to sit out state tests, I have become even more appalled by what current school policies are doing to children. The stories I have heard from parents about their children's school experiences have been even more heartbreaking than those I hear from teachers. The flood of high-stakes tests into the schools of New York State has not only turned instruction into test prep, making once-eager youngsters hate going to school, it has produced anxiety attacks and stress-related disorders on a massive scale among students as young as eight in schools around the state.

And these stories are not confined to one demographic group. I have heard them from parents in small towns, inner cities, middle-class urban neighborhoods, and suburbs. Children are traumatized by the length of the tests, by steadily growing difficulty of the material they contain and by how their teachers' jobs depend on how well they perform. And God forbid a student or a family should decide not to take the test! In more than a few school districts, children who have chosen to opt out have been browbeaten, insulted, threatened with loss of extracurricular activities and access to honors programs; told they will never get into college; told they are jeopardizing their teachers' jobs; and told they will be responsible for lowering real estate values in their neighborhood. In a few instances, they've been told they are unpatriotic and giving aid and comfort to terrorists!

Given what I have seen and heard this week from the parents of New York State, I respectfully suggest that we, as a nation, need a long period of soul-searching to examine whether the test-driven policies that are being imposed in the nation's public schools with breakneck speed are good for children. The two weeks of testing that the children of New York State are currently enduring comes perilously close to reaching abusive proportions. A society that loves and values its children would not accept this as the norm.

WEDNESDAY, APRIL 3, 2013
Why Test Resistance Is a Cause Whose Time Has Come

When people decide to resist unjust policies that have overwhelming support and for which there are few antecedents in their lifetime, they do not erupt in mass movements overnight. They are often inspired by the accumulation of individual acts of protest taken at great risk. One of the best examples of this is the lunch counter sit-ins during the civil rights movement, which began when four black college students in Greensboro, North Carolina decided to challenge segregation in their downtown business district. Their action sparked a movement in scores of cities that eventually encompassed more than thirty-five-thousand protesters, and led to the creation of the Student Nonviolent Coordinating Committee (SNCC).

We can also see this occurring during the war in Vietnam, when one of the most powerful dimensions of a movement that began with teach-ins, rallies, and marches, became draft resistance; in individuals refused induction into the military and risked imprisonment for their actions. This form of protest began in 1966 when there was a dramatic escalation of the use of US ground forces in the fighting, and became one of the most powerful weapons the antiwar movement had to awaken the conscience of the nation, as tens of thousands of young men went to prison or into exile, to show their opposition to the war.

Today I see something similar happening with the phenomenon of opting out. Parents are refusing to let their children take tests that they view as stultifying and humiliating, and students are deciding to engage in test refusal themselves. As high-stakes tests have proliferated in our public schools and are increasingly used as the basis of closing schools and firing teachers, more and more people despair of challenging policies that have bipartisan support, are championed by the media, and have the nation's economic elite pressing for their implementation. This kind of political juggernaut infuses its policies with an air of inevitability, but also gives individual acts of resistance tremendous weight. Parents who have publicly refused to let their children take tests in the face of threats from school authorities, though initially small in number, have sparked a "prairie fire" around the nation and resulted in the creation of a national organization—United Opt Out—which has become the major focal point of grassroots protest against corporate education reform. Now, you can find opt-out groups and centers of test resistance in almost every state of the union, and their examples are gradually encouraging teachers, principals, and students to join the ranks of test protesters. Even some elected officials are starting to get the message, and are championing the cause of reducing testing.

This is only the beginning. In the next few years, test resistance is likely to gather so much steam that it will force a significant reevaluation at the national, state, and local levels of policies that are making teachers hate their jobs, students hate school, and parents hate sending their children there. But this will require constant mobilization, creative organizing, and the multiplication of individual acts of courage and resistance. It also will involve local organizing that link test resisters to labor unions, religious institutions, and remnants of the Occupy movement in every town and city in the nation, and will present test resistance as a path to democratic renewal from the bottom up, fighting policies from the top down.

Monday, June 17, 2013

Why the Badass Teachers Association Has Taken Off

Over the last few years, I have founded or helped found several Facebook groups engaged in education activism and protests against corporate control of public education and the test-driven policies it has inspired. I helped create the Dump Duncan and Occupy Teach for America groups—the first two years ago and the second six months ago. Each has been dynamic and successful in promoting conversation and activism.

But nothing can compare to what has happened with a group I helped found with Midwest activist Priscilla Sanstead, called the Badass Teachers Association earlier this weekend. Within one day, the group had grown to about 270 members, and then, through a recruiting contest we organized on the recommendation of a Long Island teacher, Marla Massey Kilfoyle, membership shot up to over 1,500 members between 4 p.m. and midnight on Sunday!

The surge of energy that accompanied this meteoric rise in membership is like nothing I had experienced before in Facebook activism. And it requires some explanation. What did a group with a half-humorous and extremely provocative name do to create such excitement among teachers all over the nation? The key may lie in the statement we wrote describing our reason for creating the group: "This is for every teacher who refuses to be blamed for the failure of our society to erase poverty and inequality, and refuses to accept assessments, tests, and evaluations imposed by those who have contempt for real teaching and learning."

At a time when high-stakes testing and attacks on teacher autonomy have become official policies of both major parties, supported by the wealthiest people in the nation and cheered on by the media, teachers may have reached a tipping point regarding the campaign of demonization directed against them. The micromanagement of their classroom lives. This tipping point may have also been reached because leaders of teachers unions—who have accepted funds from groups like the Gates Foundation that support test-driven teacher evaluation—have not fought back effectively against these efforts.

Never have teachers felt more embattled, and never have they felt more alone. Many are contemplating retirement, more are under doctors' care for stress and anxiety. All fear retaliation for speaking their minds about what is happening in their districts, their schools, and their classrooms.

Now all of a sudden, a group appears that, symbolically and metaphorically, allows teachers to say: "We've had enough. We are not your doormats. We are not your punching bags. We are some of the hardest-working, most idealistic people in this country and we are not going to take it anymore.

We are going to stand up for ourselves, and stand up for our students even if no organization really supports us. We are badass. We are legion. And we will force the nation to hear our voice!"

In terms of what policies or organizing strategies will emerge from this group, only time will tell. But it is significant that there are clearly thousands of teachers in this country who are fed up with polite, respectful appeals to policy makers who hold them in contempt and are ready to fight fire with fire. In claiming the label "badass" with pride, they are announcing a new spirit of resistance, which, combined with similar movements among students and parents, could give corporate school reformers much more than they bargained for.

THURSDAY, JULY 18, 2013
Mission Statement of the Badass Teachers Association

BADASS TEACHERS ASSOCIATION
CLARIFICATION OF OUR MISSION
JULY 18, 2013

Dear Members: We would like to make it clear and concise what our mission is for this association of teachers. We believe that our actions will occur in three phases and continue to evolve as the landscape of corporate deform evolves.

Phase 1: *To call out the entities that are harming public education (corporate deformers and government officials / lawmakers). Time Frame: July / August*

Phase 2: *To educate the public about what is really going on in education policy.*

To pursue ways, prior to the start of the school year, to educate and join in partnership with parent and student groups to actively stop the privatization of our public school system. To also educate those teachers who are still in the dark about privatization efforts. Time Frame: Late July / August

Phase 3: *To continue to make public the hoax that our public school system is broken and that this is one of the many lies being spread about public education.We will actively monitor and target public figures/politicians to demand they "step up" and increase support for public education. Time Frame: Late August/Year Round*

We also want to make clear that we *are not a political organization. We do not support or endorse any political party.* The only thing that we endorse is to return public education back to the public and teacher voice to the education conversations being had at both the federal and state level.

Here is what we are clearly fighting against:

1. Badass Teachers will fight against Common Core National Standards. This stance is rooted in an extensive review of research literature, policy documents, and advice of educational historians/experts (Ravitch, Krashen, and Cody). This stance is in *NO WAY ROOTED TO SUPPORT ANY POLITICAL PARTY. BATs WILL NOT ALIGN THEMSELVES WITH ANY POLITICAL PARTY FIGHTING AGAINST CCSS. WE BELIEVE THIS IS AN "EDUCATORS" FIGHT AND WE WILL FIGHT BASED ON ITS PROPENSITY TO HARM PUBLIC EDUCATION IN AMERICA.* This group is opposed to the forced imposition of Common Core Standards on teachers, schools, and school districts. We do not exclude teachers who voluntarily work with Common Core Standards, but we vehemently oppose a one-size-fits-all model of learning that is imposed through bribery, intimidation, and extreme political pressure, for the profit of private companies, in a manner that brings with it increased testing and smothers student and teacher creativity.

2. Badass Teachers will fight against high-stakes testing and the excessive testing of our children.

3. Badass Teachers will fight against teacher evaluations tied to student test scores.

4. Badass Teachers will fight against the corporate attempt to privatize public education, which has seen the closing of schools in urban and poor areas and the subsequent opening of charter schools for profit or a voucher system that seeks to destroy neighborhood schools.

5. Badass Teachers will fight against any federal or state educational policy or mandate that has been implemented.

6.   Badass Teachers will fight against any attempt to assault, hinder, or deny our right to collective bargaining.

We hope that these six mission statements will allow you all to carry on conversations and dialogue as great badasses always do. We also hope they will provide you with a clarification of our goals. An army of 23,000 Badass Teachers will not agree on all these elements, but we do agree on most. We want to thank you all for your continued support, time, and consideration. Now let's get to work!

Respectfully your cofounders,
Mark Naison and Priscilla Sanstead
and BAT general manager
Marla Kilfoyle

Wednesday, July 24, 2013

Five Arguments to Make to New Teach for America Recruits

1.   An organization that brags about how its corps members have successful careers in investment banking after they leave teaching and actually has a formal relationship with JP Morgan is deeply problematic.
2.   An organization that takes huge amounts of money from the Walton Foundation, which is committed to privatizing public education, needs to stop promoting itself as a force for equity.
3.   An organization that tells its corps members to avoid socializing with veteran teachers or eating in the teachers' cafeteria is sending a very negative message.
4.   An organization that has a five-week training period and then sends its corps members into the most challenging classrooms in the nation's poorest neighborhoods is on dangerous ground.
5.   An organization that agrees to have its corps members as replacement labor after veteran teachers have been fired has not only relinquished the moral high ground, it has become immoral.

Part 2:

Youth Issues and Student Activism

How High School Students Helped Save the Columbia Strike— and Why the Gentrification of Manhattan Bodes Ill for the Success of Future Protests

One of the most important explanations for the length of the building occupations at Columbia in 1968, and one that I have rarely seen mentioned in histories of the event, is the role that high school students played in protecting demonstrators during the early days of the occupation.

Many commentators on the strike point out that Columbia was reluctant to bring in police to clear out demonstrators, particularly from Hamilton Hall, because of fear of provoking a riot in Harlem. But they don't really talk about why the students from the "Majority Coalition," who surrounded Hamilton Hall and Low Library during the first two days of the strike, ultimately gave up on trying to pull demonstrators out of the buildings or prevent food from getting in.

As someone who was part of the group of radical athletes and neighborhood youth who tried to get food through the Majority Coalition barricades (my girlfriend was in Hamilton Hall), I had firsthand exposure to how volatile the situation was. Majority Coalition members, several hundred in number, exchanged ugly racial epithets with the demonstrators in Hamilton Hall, and tried to punch and tackle members of our Food Committee when we broke their barricade around Low Library.

99

But it was not members of our fifteen-person "SDS Goon Squad" that persuaded the Majority Coalition to end their barricade around the occupied buildings; it was the group of five hundred high school students from Harlem and the West Side who confronted opponents of the strike on the third day of the occupation. The majority of these students came from Brandeis High School, a notoriously tough school located on Eighty-Fourth Street between Columbus and Amsterdam Avenues, located in what was then a working-class, mostly Puerto Rican neighborhood. As they marched through the Broadway and Amsterdam Avenue gates onto the campus chanting Black Power slogans, many of the Majority Coalition students began to think twice about whether they were willing to get involved in what could easily turn into a race war with neighborhood teenagers. From that point on, the demonstrators no longer had to worry about their fellow students; police action that became their major concern.

Why is it important to emphasize this incident? Because without the passionate support of people in the working-class black and Latino communities adjoining Columbia, the strike and occupations would not have lasted seven days and would not have produced the major policy change the strike induced—halting construction of the gym in Morningside Heights.

Sadly, many of those working-class neighborhoods are gone. The blocks surrounding Brandeis have become prime Manhattan real estate, with some of the highest rents in the city. Manhattan Valley, the tough, mostly Puerto Rican area bordered by Amsterdam Avenue, Central Park West, 110th Street, and 100th Street is gentrifying at breakneck speed, only saved from a complete turnover in population by the public housing project on its borders. And Harlem is in the midst of a development boom that is radically changing its racial and class composition.

Today, should Columbia students decide to seize buildings on their campus in support of an important objective, whether stopping Columbia's expansion or ending the war in Iraq, one would be hard pressed to find or mobilize a critical mass of high school students living close enough to the campus to influence university policy. And as for the people of Harlem rioting to defend their community from outside forces—as they did to protest police brutality in 1935, 1943, and 1965—that I am afraid, is something the class and racial diversity of the neighborhood has rendered most unlikely.

Without worrying about pressure and possible violence from residents of neighborhoods outside the campus, the Columbia administration will have a relatively free hand to deal with its own students if they protest university policies. That is why the current university expansion plan, unlike the gym project in Morningside Park, is likely to go forward with little opposition.

THURSDAY, DECEMBER 4, 2008

The Crisis of African American and Latino Male Youth: A Bronx Perspective

This essay was presented at the CUNY Black Male Initiative Inaugural Conference, April 26, 2006.

It would be a daunting task to give a historical overview of the position of black men in American society. Even if I were John Hope Franklin, I don't think I could summarize the impact of slavery, Jim Crow, deindustrialization, and the rise of the prison-industrial complex.

Instead, this essay will focus on my own research on African American communities in the Bronx in the 1940s and 1950s, and analyze how the position of black men in those communities offers insights and possible lessons for reengaging young black men with the educational system and the mainstream economy.

The two communities I have been studying have been Morrisania—which emerged as the Bronx's largest African American neighborhood as a result of a massive migration from Harlem in the 1940s—and the Patterson Houses, the Bronx's first low-income public housing development which opened in 1950. In the last three and a half years, with the help of a team of community researchers, I have done more than 150 oral history interviews with people who moved to, or grew up in, those two communities in the 1940s and 1950s, and collected photos and documents that bring to life the stories told in those interviews.

The image that emerges with overwhelming force from interviews and documents is of strong, cohesive neighborhoods where working-class black and Latino residents looked out for one another, shared their cultures, raised one another's children, and looked to the future with considerable optimism. In 1951, an African American magazine called *Our World* described Morrisania in terms that almost no one today would apply to black or Latino neighborhoods in the Bronx: "Right now, most of the Bronx's 75,000 Negroes live between 160th Street and Crotona Park South. To them, the Bronx is a borough of hope, a place of unlimited possibilities."

African American men played a central role in creating this atmosphere of security and hope. The majority of adult men in these communities were in families and in the labor force and black men played key roles as mentors to local youth in churches, community centers, and after-school and night centers in the public schools. Most of the people I interviewed have spoken of the influence of ministers, teachers, community center directors, and their own fathers in guiding them through the sometimes-perilous pathway to adulthood. Figures like Reverend Edler Hawkins of St. Augustine Presbyterian Church; Floyd Lane of the PS 18 night center; Vincent Tibbs of the PS 99 night center; Eddie Bonnamere, a music teacher at Clark Junior High School and Hilton White, who ran a community basketball program at 163rd Street and Caldwell Avenue, are mentioned in interview after interview as people who saved lives and inspired others to achieve more than they ever dreamed possible.

These working-class black and Latino neighborhoods, were not without problems—they had gangs, alcoholism, and heavily tracked schools. But adult black men were a powerful presence in families, voluntary institutions, and publicly funded recreation programs, and they passed on a legacy of strength, optimism, and community responsibility to young men in the next generation, some of whom went on to careers in civil service, teaching, social work, health professions, the media, politics, and business.

However, even in these relatively optimistic times, racism in the city's labor and housing markets were chipping away at the stability of these neighborhoods, and undermining the ability of black and Latino families to accumulate social capital and transfer it successfully to the next generation. With few exceptions, the portraits of black fathers that emerge from the interviews is of men who worked two or three jobs in the most fragile sectors of the secondary labor market. They drove cabs, loaded trucks, worked in factories and cleaning establishments, operated elevators, cleaned buildings, and worked as cooks and porters on trains. Although there was a small component of government workers (especially postal workers and people who worked for New York City transit) and a few people who owned small businesses, skilled unionized workers in the construction, printing, or garment trades are strikingly absent, especially in comparison to Jewish, Irish, and Italian neighborhoods at the time.

In the 1950s and even into the 1960s, New York had tens of thousands of high-paying, unionized, blue-collar jobs that could be passed on from father to son and elevate a family into the middle class, and black men had virtually none of these jobs! The worst example of this was the construction trades. Even though many black men came from the South and from the West Indies with construction skills, they could not get jobs as electricians, plumbers, steamfitters, or sheet metal workers on major construction projects, even when those projects were located in black neighborhoods. The following is a quote from Oliver Leeds, a leader of Brooklyn CORE who led massive sit-ins during the construction of Downstate Medical Center in 1963 (this comes courtesy of my colleague Brian Purnell, who is writing a dissertation on the history of the civil rights movement in Brooklyn):

> I went in the Army and I tried to join the Tank Corps. When I got to Louisiana, I found I was in the Corps of Engineers. And you know what we do? We worked to win the war. We built anything that could be built: bridges, tunnels, houses, officers' quarters, mess quarters, roads, airstrips. We loaded and unloaded ships. We did anything in the way that involved work, construction work. You know when I got back to the United States, after the war, I couldn't get a job in construction, and there was no union that would let me in. And there was damn little that I couldn't do in the way of construction work. They'll take you and turn you into construction workers in the army, in a segregated army, and then when you get back into civilian life, you can't get a construction job.

The corrosive effect of this discrimination is visible in several ways. Most black men had to work two or three secondary labor market jobs to make the salary of a single unionized construction worker, making the task of supporting their families far more stressful than for their Irish, Italian, or Jewish counterparts. Black men had no marketable craft skills, or union connections, to pass on to their children. And the blue-collar jobs that black men did have were, unlike construction, vulnerable to elimination as the city shifted from an industrial to a finance, information-based economy.

This had devastating consequences for black families and communities. Basically, from the 1950s through the 1970s, a period when the city's economy was losing hundreds of thousands of industrial jobs, African Americans, unlike their Jewish, Irish, or Italian counterparts, could not attain upward mobility within the working class, or achieve middle-class incomes through blue-collar occupations. Indeed, black male youth who did not graduate from college actually faced worse employment prospects than their fathers, because many of the jobs their fathers worked were being eliminated.

This helped trigger a fragmentation of the social structure of working-class black and Latino communities like Morrisania or the Patterson Houses. As college-educated and upwardly mobile families from these communities moved to the North and East Bronx, Queens, Westchester, or New Jersey, men who remained, who for the most part had high school educations or less, faced an economy that offered them lower wages and even more humiliating conditions of work than their fathers had experienced. For many, the underground economy was their only realistic option, but this was not the relatively benign, nonviolent, underground economy of their father's day, which was organized around the numbers business. This was the fierce high-stakes heroin trade of Nicky Barnes and Guy Fisher, which left corpses, broken lives, and shattered communities in its wake. In this fierce and frightening atmosphere, being a husband, father, and family man was an overwhelming strain on even the best-intentioned young man and many cracked under the strain. Many young men weren't up to it, a tragedy presented with great power in the Hughes brothers' brilliant movie *Dead Presidents*.

To make matters worse, as the job crunch on young working-class black men intensified and the violence of their daily lives became more overwhelming, New York City underwent a fiscal crisis. With the help of the Emergency Financial Control Board, the city's politicians decided that youth mentoring and recreation was expendable. All the after-school and night centers in New York public schools were shut down, recreation supervisors were removed from the parks, and the great music programs in the city's junior high schools were eliminated. So at a time when young men needed them the most, the Floyd Lanes, Vincent Tibbses, Eddie Bonnameres, and Hilton Whites were removed as forces in Bronx neighborhoods and other places like them around the city.

By the beginning of the 1980s, the idea of cohesive, safe, working-class black and Latino communities in the South Bronx with a strong male presence in families and the legal labor force had become unimaginable to people growing up in those neighborhoods. They faced a world of mean streets, shattered families, and a legal labor market that offered them little but stagnant wages and a humiliating work culture. And that was before crack!

The world we live in now, one where young black men feel so alienated and marginalized, has been shaped by many historical forces, some of them going back to slavery. But many of the problems have roots in labor market discrimination in the relatively recent past, and in shortsighted and pernicious government policies implemented less than thirty years ago.

Fifty years ago, black men were a central part of every formal and informal institution in South Bronx neighborhoods, and were an integral in the leadership structure that made these communities safe and cohesive. If we change government priorities, challenge racial hierarchies in the labor market, and make mentoring programs in schools and neighborhoods part of the daily life of children and adolescents, there is no reason why they cannot play that role again.

The Streets Are Still Part
of Bronx Hip-Hop

This was a speech given at the Conference on Hip-Hop and Street Culture in Barcelona, Spain, June 2, 2008.

> "He knows the code. It's not about a salary
> It's about reality and making some noise"
> —Fort Minor, "Remember the Name"

Last October, when I was taking a group of people on a tour of the Bronx's historic black neighborhood Morrisania, I noticed a group of twenty teenagers standing in a circle on the corner of 168th Street and Prospect Avenue, clapping their hands in rhythm, while one by one, people entered the circle and began dancing energetically and acrobatically. I watched for a minute in my car and then drove off to my next destination, thinking that the street dance tradition that began in the Bronx in the 1970s, which people called "b-boying," or breakdancing, seemed to have gotten a new lease on life. My curiosity piqued, I kept a close eye peeled for street dancing on all my drives through Bronx neighborhoods and saw the same kind of circular gathering on Bronx street corners at least three more times. I also noticed, during my visits to Bronx schools where I regularly give lectures, that every single musical performance or talent show that I saw featured dance moves that seemed a cross between those being done in contemporary hip-hop videos and routines from 1980s breakdancing films.

The vitality of street dance traditions in Bronx neighborhoods impressed me so much that I mentioned it during a lecture to teachers at a public university in the Bronx last month, only to be told that the dance phenomenon that I saw actually had a name—"Getting Lite"—and that it was being done by informal dance crews all over the Bronx who were posting their performances on YouTube.

When I got home, I decided to explore this phenomenon and found an incredible array of "Getting Lite" videos in settings that varied from school cafeterias, to street corners, to apartment living rooms, to the insides of McDonald'ses, Burger Kings, and other fast-food joints. The dancers were black and Latino, male and female, and were in their early to middle teens, with the average age being thirteen or fourteen. The moves they were doing involved very rapid and graceful foot movements, occasionally accompanied by dips and spins, but the dances lacked the aggressive upper-body component of early breakdancing and "krumping"—a contemporary dance craze that started on the West Coast—and seemed easier to do in a confined space. They were also less gender exclusive—a good number of the dancers in "Getting Lite" videos were young women. The videos themselves were relatively primitive, probably taken on cell phones, but the participants still managed to post them on the Internet where some of them registered thousands of hits. Here was electronic democracy at work; giving young people the opportunity to showcase their skills to thousands of people instantly, with minimal expense.

As someone who has been studying the cultural and musical traditions of the Bronx, the emergence of a new dance style in some of the very neighborhoods where breakdancing originated thirty years ago fascinated me. Like hip-hop itself during its early years, roughly 1973–76, Getting Lite began as a grassroots youth movement in Bronx neighborhoods without any encouragement from commercial media. While amateur Getting Lite videos are all over the Internet, the dance has not yet been acknowledged or publicized on the major music television networks—MTV and BET—and has not been incorporated into a commercially distributed hip-hop video.

That a cultural movement can still start "from the bottom up" in Bronx neighborhoods raises interesting questions on the continuing salience of urban public spaces as centers of cultural and musical creativity. Is this something unique to the Bronx, or does it exist wherever large number of marginalized people live in crowded conditions, and where immigration and internal migrations bring people with different cultural traditions in close proximity to one another?

The Bronx today, as it was sixty years ago, when rhythm and blues, jazz, and Afro-Cuban music were the sounds heard on the streets; and as it was thirty years ago, when hip-hop jams were capturing the imagination of young people in schoolyards, community centers, and parks; is a multicultural urban space being rapidly transformed by people of various ethnicities moving into the borough in search of affordable housing. According to the University Neighborhood Housing Program, the Bronx, which has the lowest rents in the city and the highest number of rent-stabilized apartments, has become the borough of choice for "the poorest households who can no longer find an affordable apartment in other parts of the city."

Many of these households are composed of recent immigrants, particularly from West Africa, Mexico, and the Dominican Republic, who are moving into private rental housing in the southern and western portions of the borough. Statistically, the Bronx has the highest rates of severe overcrowding in the city—4.5 percent compared to the citywide average of 3.7 percent. But those rates, based on government surveys, are notoriously unreliable when dealing with undocumented immigrants, and seriously underestimate the extent of the problem.

A South Bronx priest that I interviewed, Reverend John Grange, pointed to the block of five-story tenements across the street from his church and said that there was an entire Mexican family, often composed of six or seven people, living in every single room in those buildings. Anyone walking or driving along major Bronx thoroughfares like Fordham Road, the Grand Concourse, Tremont Avenue, East 138th Street, or trying to find a parking place on the street in many Bronx neighborhoods, is likely to trust Father Grange's estimates more than those of the US Census. The Bronx below Fordham Road is packed with people, all of them black and brown and most of them working-class and poor, who represent a wide variety of nationalities, religions, and cultural traditions. Every day, it seems a new mosque, Mexican restaurant, a Dominican grocery or hair-braiding store opens up, and school classrooms are filled with children speaking a wide variety of languages and dialects, including Soninke, Malinke, and Bambara, rarely been spoken in the United States, and only taught in a handful of universities.

What does this have to do with hip-hop culture and Getting Lite? In my opinion, quite a bit. For many young people growing up in the Bronx today, the streets may represent one of the freer, and ironically, safer social spaces they can congregate in. Crowded households, with people sleeping in shifts, boarders renting space, and new family members moving in until they can find their own living quarters, can be stress-filled, noisy, and sometimes violent—hardly places young people would go to seek refuge from danger or find peace and quiet.

In my own oral history interviews with Bronx residents, especially those growing up in working-class neighborhoods in the '70s, '80s, and '90s family violence was a recurring theme, as it was in Adrian Nicole Leblanc's celebrated book *Random Family*, which deals with Bronx residents immersed in the drug business, and Ivan Sanchez's recently published memoir *Last Stop: Growing Up Wild Style in the Bronx*. Poverty, crowding, substance abuse, domestic violence, and the cultural dissonance that can separate generations in immigrant families are factors that pushed generations of Bronx youngsters to seek refuge in the streets, and many are still doing so today.

If you look at the Getting Lite videos, what comes across most strongly is the unalloyed joy that the dancers display in showing their skills. There are huge smiles on the faces of the kids entering the circle to dance and on the faces of those clapping while they perform. It makes me wonder: Do the people in those videos ever look that happy while they are in school or when they are in their apartments? Is there anything else they do that makes them feel so free and so alive? There is also considerable diversity in the young people participating. There are girls as well as boys, Latinos as well as blacks, and, if I can read appearance and body language accurately, kids whose families come from Africa as well as the South and the West Indies. Family problems, language problems, money problems, test-passing problems (stemming from schools obsessed with standardized test scores) all seem erased by joyous participation in spontaneous performances that young people create by themselves for themselves, in spaces designed for other uses.

The exuberant atmosphere of the Getting Lite circles, whose participants perform for "street credibility" and neighborhood fame rather than financial gain, mirrors that of the outdoor jams that helped create hip-hop culture in the Bronx in the 1970s. To quote David Toop (from James Spady's book *Street Conscious Rap*): "In those early days, each DJ was strong in his own district and was supported by local followers. Few had access to the big clubs so the venues were block parties and schools, or in the summer, the parks. A party in the park would entail wiring the sound system to a lamp post or going to the house nearest the park, paying the owner and running a cable to their electricity. Then the party would go on till the police broke it up."

A more detailed portrait of one of the most popular outdoor venues for Bronx hip-hop, "'63 Park," a schoolyard at the intersection of Boston Road and 169th Street—only six blocks from where I first saw Getting Lite dances—is provided by Sheri Sher in a novel called *Mercedes Ladies,* about her own experiences with Bronx hip-hop:

> Boston Road was the place to be, especially during the summer months, because you always had different DJ crews playing music on the corner. The block was always rocking. Come on, with Grandmaster Flash and the Furious Five, Grand Wizard Theodore and the L Brothers, Kool Herc and the Herculords . . . Boston Road in the Bronx was one of the original home bases for hip hop. We'd just be rockin' on the street corners or in '63 Park, which was actually a concrete schoolyard down the block. Wherever the music was playing, everybody would be out there. The streets used to be packed, especially during the summer months. Speakers were big as hell with amps to match. They'd be plugged into the street lamppost, or the electric cord extension would be coming from somebody's house through the window. People danced in the streets or simply stood around posting while the music blasted . . . . If you're a real hip-hop head, you can imagine the electricity that was in the atmosphere. This went on until either the power went out or you heard gunshots from somewhere. Then the cops would come shut shit down. All this action fell under the heading of street jams; they were like a free concert without any promoters or salaries involved, held purely for street rep and fun. It was always a carefree atmosphere.

Though some of the terms Sheri Sher used to describe the jams as "'63 Park"—"carefree atmosphere," "purely for street rep and fun"—could be applied to Getting Lite circles today, the social conditions in Bronx neighborhoods in the '70s were, at least on the surface, far more dismal. Huge portions of the housing stock of the South Bronx were burning in those years, leaving a landscape filled with rubble-strewn lots, burned-out cars and vacant apartment buildings with broken windows. Hip-hop jams, held in community centers, schoolyards, and the open areas of public housing projects, provided temporary escape from the surrounding chaos.

A verse from Grandmaster Flash's "The Message" —"can't take the smell/can't take the noise/got no money to move out/you know I've got no choice"—spoke for a generation of young people in the Bronx who attended early hip-hop events. During an oral history interview, Joe Conzo Jr., hip-hop's first photographer, described sitting by his window in a public housing project and watching the tenements across the street, on Caldwell Avenue north of 156th Street, burn to the ground. Matthew Swain, a computer programmer today, described his relief at moving from Andrews Avenue in the West Bronx, where many of the buildings were burning, to the Mill Brook Houses, a public housing project in the South Bronx, where DJs spun records in the park every summer and where fires were no longer a threat. In those difficult years, hip-hop was a gesture of defiance and affirmation by young people living in communities that had been abandoned by private capital and government, and had been written off as dead by most of the outside world.

But if the physical landscape of the Bronx is very different today than it was in the '70s—most of the burned-out sections have been cleaned out and filled with townhouses, apartment buildings, and strip malls—young people living in the borough are still coping with extreme stress. Living in crowded neighborhoods filled with recent immigrants and people pushed out of Brooklyn and Manhattan, young people growing up in the Bronx today are as poor, and as hypersegregated, as their counterparts were thirty years ago. While public services, especially police and fire protection have improved, and levels of public violence are considerably lower, recreation services for youth have lagged far behind new housing construction. Young people, once they reach adolescence, have few opportunities for creative activity once school hours are over. In this setting, the streets still beckon, and hip-hop culture, which provides a nonviolent, celebratory outlet for youthful artistry and rebelliousness, offers a powerful reminder of the potential and resilient spirit of Bronx's young people who have found their own way to resist the many forces trying to render them invisible. So get on your Internet browser, type in "Getting Lite in the Bronx" and prepare yourself for a treat! Like their counterparts thirty years ago, the kids "Getting Lite," with the help of new technologies, may have created something that will spark a response among young people in similar circumstances all around the world.

Hustling, Schools, and the Education of Inner-City Boys— Reflections on a Talk by Street Lit Author Jihad Uhuru

Jihad Uhuru's talk in our Hip-Hop Street Lit Narratives class last week helped me understand some very important issues—one of which is the failure of schools to engage working-class students of color, particularly boys. Jihad, a very successful "street lit" author, was one of those boys who found nothing in school to connect with. Even though he had black teachers, even though black notables came to his school to talk about their successes and inspire students to emulate them, and even though he was clearly incredibly intelligent, Jihad was stubbornly resistant to reading and any form of academic engagement. It was only when he went to prison in his late teens that he immersed himself in books. It was only then that he became immersed in reading, and discovered that history and philosophy and political theory could help him make sense of the world and his own place in it.

As Jihad described his experiences, it became clear to me that the environment he grew up in, during the late '70s and early '80s, was very different from the black, inner city communities I had spent time in during the late '60s. First of all, political revolutionaries were no longer a presence. They were not giving speeches on street corners, selling their newspapers outside the convenience store, or talking about black unity and revolution at the dinner table or in the barber shop. But something else, maybe something even more important, was also missing from Jihad's life; black men who went to work in the morning, and came back at night after working a long hard day with money in their pocket, and the satisfaction of a job well done. Those kinds of black men were still highly visible in inner city neighborhoods in the late '60s—they worked in steel mills and auto factories, drove trucks and buses, and owned their own cabs and the like. But by the time Jihad was growing up, the black male working class was fast disappearing as a force in inner city neighborhoods. The only black people making good money, legally, were people with college degrees working in white-collar occupations, and they were moving out of inner city neighborhoods into the suburbs.

So, what kind of black men did Jihad see and interact with during his childhood and adolescence? To an extraordinary extent, the black men Jihad was meeting, interacting with, and modeling himself on, including his own father, were getting most of their income in the underground economy and living lives that occasionally offered great rewards, but also involved danger and instability. I think we need to probe the implications of this economic transformation.

What does it meant to grow up in a neighborhood where the primary source of work and income, at least for men, is illegal activity? In the neighborhood Jihad grew up in, "hustling" was more than just a source of income, it was a whole way of life with its own language, forms of dress, gender roles, and family dynamics. Men who made their money illegally were at constant risk of imprisonment and death, and were unlikely to commit themselves to the kind of stable family relationships that someone who worked in a steel mill or an auto plant might have been drawn to. They moved in and out of relationships with women, and had only tangential relationships to the children they fathered.

In addition, their ways of earning income seemed to have little relationship to books or to the disciplined learning environments schools tried to provide. What made men successful in the underground economy was bravery, quick thinking, and capacity to persuade and inspire using language that barely resembled the vocabulary offered in third-grade reading or social studies. Hustlers communicated through an insider's language that was indecipherable to most middle-class people, whether black or white. But it was that language that was the language of money, the language of success, and the language of power in the neighborhood Jihad grew up in!

As a bright male child growing up in an environment where most of the money came from illegal activities, and where the men involved in those activities dressed, spoke, and carried themselves in a way that bore no resemblance to anything presented in school, Jihad naturally concluded that school had no relevance to someone like him. Money, power, respect, in his neighborhood, and in his family—at least for boys—came through mastery of the hustlers' code, the hustlers' language, the hustlers' lifestyle, and ultimately, through recruitment into the alternative economy that hustlers had created.

Once a young man has the realization that the street economy is going to be his only path to money and respect and the good things in life—and for some this can happen as early as age eight—teachers are facing an uphill battle to get them engaged in reading, writing, and math, especially since the language used in teaching those subjects, whether in readers, or on tests, is totally different from the language of the street economy.

What you have then is a battle of language loyalties with the teacher on one side, and the hustlers the young men aspire to be on the other, and that is a battle the teacher will usually lose. This isn't because the hustlers' language is "blacker" or more "authentic," but because in the young person's neighborhood, the hustlers' language is the language of *success*.

From the outside, we may think that turning off school, for a young person who grew up the way Jihad did, is shortsighted and self-destructive. But given the limited opportunities for employment in the legal economy that he saw in his neighborhood and family, looking to the hustling culture rather than school as the place to invest his energies may be a rational decision.

If this analysis is correct, we are going to face an uphill battle in trying to get inner-city boys to become engaged in school unless we can rebuild and reconstruct legal economic opportunities for men of color that equal those offered by hustling and the underground economy.

Children look at what they see around them and decide, fairly early, what works and what doesn't. And in many neighborhoods around this country, there is no evidence, especially for boys, that school leads to economic opportunities for people like them. Until that changes, don't expect school reform to accomplish very much.

FRIDAY, NOVEMBER 20, 2009

Violence in a Familiar Place: Young People Left Behind in Morrisania's Housing Renaissance

When I picked up the paper two days ago and read about the shooting of Vada Vasquez on a Bronx street corner, I felt a chill go through me. Not only was it depressing to read about another young person hit by a stray bullet in an inner-city neighborhood—there have been too many such stories in recent weeks—but the corner the shooting took place on, Home Street and Prospect Avenue, is one I have driven by hundreds of times and walked through at least twenty times when leading tours of historic Morrisania for teachers, student groups, and visitors from abroad.

This particular shooting took place in the heart of what was once the Bronx's largest and most dynamic black community, a place that hummed with vitality in the 1940s, '50s, and '60s and produced an unmatched variety of poplar music ranging from jazz, to mambo, to doo-wop, to salsa and funk. Even in the '70s, when the neighborhood was devastated by fires, young people living in it helped create a new music form—hip-hop— which eventually became the voice of disenfranchised young people throughout the world. Today, Morrisania is still a center of musical creativity, with new groups of immigrants from Africa, Mexico, and the Dominican Republic fusing their musical cultures with hip-hop and R&B. The very corner on which Vada Vasquez was shot, Home and Prospect, was the first place I saw young people in the Bronx performing a new kind of street dance that they had created called "Getting Lite."

But all of this wonderful history meant little when I thought of Vada Vasquez, lying on life support in a local hospital, or the sixteen-year-old Carvett Gentles who allegedly shot her, who may spend most of his life in jail. Why did this tragedy take place? And why was hardly anybody who lives in Morrisania surprised that something like this happened?

Some of the blame for this shooting has to be assigned to the easy availability of guns on the streets of New York, many of them brought in from states like Virginia, that make it as easy to buy a gun as it is to buy a portable CD player. But much of it has to be attributed to the misguided priorities of those who have controlled community economic development in the New York City.

From the outside, the neighborhood Vada Vasquez was shot in looks like a great New York City success story. If you walk ten blocks in any direction from the corner of Prospect and Home, you will see literally thousands of units of new residential housing placed on what were once vacant lots, some of them townhouses, some of them apartment buildings, most of them built in the last five years.

When I first encountered this wave of new construction several years ago, I was inclined to see it as a kind of Bronx Renaissance until Leroi Archible, a longtime Bronx activist and one of the wisest men I know said to me, "Mark, what are they going to do with all the kids who are going to leave here? They haven't built a single youth center or recreation facility along with all the housing. Those kids are all going to be out in the street and getting into trouble."

More prophetic words have rarely been uttered. With thousands of units of new housing going up in Morrisania, virtually all of them being occupied by families with young children, why hasn't someone in city planning or Housing Preservation and Development seen fit to make sure at least one new youth center, either operated by the city or a nonprofit organization, is built in the neighborhood?

Worse yet, why haven't local elected officials pressed the Department of Education to keep every school in the neighborhood—and there are at least ten within walking distance of Home and Prospect—open from 3 p.m. to 10 p.m. with arts, sports, and supervised recreation?

Morrisania is a neighborhood filled with teenagers who have nothing to do when they leave school. There are no jobs, in part because there are almost no stores, no sports programs, no art programs, and there are no places where they can congregate under adult supervision.

Should anyone be surprised if they hang out on the streets, sell drugs, join gangs? What else do they have to do? Where else do they have to go?

It's time that policy makers at all levels make youth issues a top priority when planning and carrying out community economic development. First of all, whenever large numbers of housing units are placed in a particular neighborhood, youth centers should offer free sports and arts programs to local children and adolescents should be built. I am going to establish an arbitrary ratio, say five thousand units of new housing equal one youth center. Let's make this official city policy.

Secondly, every school in New York City should be open from 3 p.m. to 9 p.m. for supervised recreation under the direction of licensed public school teachers. This is what we had fifty years ago in New York, and we need to bring this program back. Our young people desperately need mentors like Vincent Tibbs, who ran the night center at PS 99, only two blocks from Prospect and Home. Tibbs influenced thousands of Morrisania's young people to stay in school and keep out of trouble. As a model for the rest of the city, let's open a Vincent Tibbs Center in PS 99, and invite all the young people in the neighborhood to use it on a regular basis. I'll bet if we do that there will be a lot less shootings.

Finally, let's bring back the recreation supervisors in the city's vest pocket parks, positions that were eliminated in the '70s, which we desperately need today. Fifty years ago, just ten blocks from Prospect and Home, a "Parkie" named Hilton White ran a community basketball program that served hundreds of youngsters and sent scores of its graduates to college, including three of the starters on the Texas Western team that won the NCAA Championship in 1966. Our young people need mentors like Hilton White even more now than they did then. Bring the Parkies back!

The policies I am suggesting all cost money. But no more than the money it takes to put and keep young people in prison. It's time we invest in young people before they turn to acts of violence. If we don't, we are going to read more and more stories about broken dreams and wasted lives.

Building New Housing Without Youth Centers and Stores Doesn't Create Community—Reflections on a Walking Tour of Morrisania

Last Wednesday, I led a walking tour of Morrisania for twenty-five interns from a community legal services organizations called "The Bronx Defenders." The group, mostly consisting of law students, was young, sharp, and keenly observant. The tour is one of my favorite events, as it gives me a chance to talk about Morrisania's unique history. The community is one of the most racially and cultural integrated communities in the United States, from the late 1930s through the early 1960s, and can boast an unmatched legacy of musical creativity. The tour also gives me a chance to talk about the arson and abandonment cycle that hit the neighborhood in the late sixties and lasted through the late seventies, leading to a loss of nearly half the neighborhood's housing stock and nearly 60 percent of its population by the 1980.

Despite the tragic events the tour covers, it usually ends on a somewhat upbeat note because of the wave of new housing construction taking place in Morrisania. Each time I do the tour, it seems that another vacant lot is being filled with two- or three-family townhouses, or six- to eight-story apartment buildings, to the point where there are almost no vacant lots left. Even during the current economic crisis, the rebuilding of Morrisania's housing stock has continued unabated, with new construction being initiated someplace in the neighborhood almost weekly.

But though this wave of new construction is certainly gratifying, especially to someone who lived in the neighborhood or who visited it regularly during those terrifying years when huge stretches of Morrisania and nearby Hunts Point offered a depressing vista of garbage-filled lots, abandoned cars, and wild dogs roaming the streets, there were some critical things missing amidst what some people would consider a miracle of urban revitalization.

One of these is youth centers. During our three-mile walk through Morrisania, going through the neighborhood's major thoroughfares (Stebbins Avenue, Prospect Avenue, Boston Road, 163rd Street) as well as many side streets, we saw what had to be several thousand new units of affordable housing, but not one new gymnasium, Boys and Girls Club, PAL Center, or YMCA/YWCA.

To many members of my tour group, this seemed like an example of incredibly poor planning. Bringing thousands of new residents into a neighborhood, many of whom are young immigrant families with children, without making any provision for indoor recreation space or organized sports leagues for children and adolescents was a virtual invitation to these youngsters to spend their leisure hours in the street. In a community that already had a serious gang problem and a thriving drug economy, this was a prescription for disaster. Several people we met in the neighborhood, like longtime Bronx youth worker and neighborhood advocate Hetty Fox, said that the absence of constructive youth activities had created a vicious cycle of drug-related violence and brutal, often indiscriminate police harassment that made life in Morrisania extremely dangerous and stressful for neighborhood adolescents, especially adolescent males. She spoke of the "genius of youth" being wasted in her community, and called the destruction of human potential taking place in the Bronx just as bad, if not worse, as the destruction of the borough's housing stock in the 1970s.

Shaken by Fox's comments, our group looked at all the newly built housing we passed with more cynical eyes and noticed something else missing—stores and commercial space. Frankly, this was something I had never noticed before on my walks through the neighborhood, but the group's observation was right on point. There are large portions of Morrisania, most notably along Stebbins Avenue (now Reverend James Polite Place) where scores of new multiple dwellings had been erected without so much as a single grocery store being opened to serve what were probably thousands of new residents. The same was true of new housing built along Home Street, Union Avenue, and other secondary thoroughfares. Not only did such an absence of commercial development make shopping more time consuming and inconvenient for Morrisania residents, it missed an opportunity to spur the creation of small businesses, which promote sociability among old and new residents, an outlet for ethnic enterprise, and create legal job opportunities for neighbor-hood youth.

By the time we had finished our Morrisania tour—at a great neigh-borhood small business called Johnson's BBQ, in the same location for over fifty years—we were all feeling that a huge opportunity had been missed to recreate the nurturing atmosphere and community spirit that Morrisania had possessed in the 1940s, 1950s, and 1960s. In their rush to fill the city's desperate need for affordable housing, city officials and local community groups had neglected to provide room in their plans for two critical com-ponents of a healthy city neighborhood—youth programs and small busi-nesses. The result was a neighborhood that on the surface looked healthy and dynamic, but was plagued with drug-related violence and a sense of trepidation among many residents about what would happen to their chil-dren when they reached adolescence.

It's time we start doing the kind of holistic planning that my good friend Leroi Archible (known throughout the Bronx as "Street Man") has been recommending for years and start building youth centers, ball fields, and strip malls in every portion of the Bronx marked off for "redevelop-ment." Throwing up housing without other services and amenities is a poor prescription for creating community.

TUESDAY, DECEMBER 20, 2011
The Sixties Student Movement and the Working Class—Clearing Up Misconceptions

During the 1960s, New York City was the scene of an incredibly powerful antiwar and student movement. Like Occupy Wall Street, this movement was often attacked for being unrepresentative of the city's working class. In reality, it was far more diverse in class and race than critics or historians realized at the time. As a participant in this movement and a historian trying to make sense of it, I want to give a sense of how important the working-class component of the antiwar and student movements in New York City were in the 1960s and early 70s. In doing so, I will present some rarely discussed features of the Columbia strike, the most publicized of student movements during the period the struggle for open admissions at the City University; antiwar activism in the city's high schools; and neighborhood organizing projects spawned by SDS, the Black Panther Party, and the Young Lords Party.

The Columbia strike, a building occupation that lasted seven days, has often been held up as a prototypical example of elite leadership of the student movement and the antiwar movement. This is not entirely wrong. The vast majority of the leadership and membership of Columbia SDS, along with the majority of the white students who occupied four of the five buildings, were from middle-class and upper-middle-class families. However, the black students who occupied Hamilton Hall, without whose leadership and militancy the "occupation" strategy would have never been introduced, were far more diverse in class origins than SDS members. Many of the students occupying Hamilton Hall, including my own girlfriend at the time, came from working-class and lower-middle-class families, products of a new admissions policy which Columbia had introduced beginning in 1966 that multiplied the number of black students at the school more than six-fold. In addition, leaders from Harlem organizations were regular participants in the Hamilton Hall occupation, giving the entire movement space to operate because Columbia administrators were afraid they might cause rioting in Harlem and lead to attacks on the university, especially if police actiona reversed to pull Hamilton Hall occupants out. In addition, high school students from Harlem and the Upper West Wide played a major roles in the strike when they marched, five hundred strong, onto the Columbia campus to break through a blockade of the buildings that conservative athletes had set up to try to "starve out" protesters.

Without a highly politicized Harlem community, and strong student movements in largely working-class New York City high schools, which mobilized in support of black student occupiers and the movement as a whole, the Columbia strike would have likely ended in one or two days. Its most important victory—the prevention of the construction of a private gymnasium for Columbia students in a public park adjoining the campus would not have been acheived.

But though the Columbia strike was the most publicized student movement in that era in New York City and the nation, it was far surpassed by an entirely working-class movement—the struggle for open admissions at the City University of New York (CUNY). In 1969 black and Latino students at City College initiated a strike and blockaded the school to demand that the overwhelming white four-year colleges of CUNY open their doors to students of color who had become the majority in the city's high schools. This fierce battle, supported by SDS chapters around the city, won an incredible victory. The City University board voted to radically change admissions standards for its four-year colleges, and initiate a broad-based remediation program to accommodate the new students. The results were astonishing. Within one year, the number of freshmen attending CUNY four-year colleges rose from 20,000 to 35,000, and the number of students of color tripled. This was arguably the greatest single victory won by the student movement in New York City during the entire period, and was organized and led by students from working-class backgrounds.

Where did these students come from? How were they politicized? Here we have to look at the impact of black students organizations founded in the city's high schools and colleges, as well as the impact of community organizing and political education carried on by the Nation of Islam and the Black Panther Party. When Stokely Carmichael of SNCC launched the Black Power slogan, it captured the imagination of black students around the nation. The idea that Black people had to create separate organizations to achieve true self-determination touched a particular chord with black students at predominantly white institutions, and led to the formation of black student unions on every City University campus and at private colleges like Columbia, NYU, and Fordham. The college black student unions, in turn, reached out to black students at public high schools to form student organizations of their own—a process that was often resisted by recalcitrant administrators who demanded that black history be taught as part of the curriculum. The result was considerable political turmoil at the city high schools around issues of race and representation, which was only increased by the 1968 teachers strike, which pitted community groups in black and Latino neighborhoods seeking local control of all aspects of school management against a teachers union determined to control hiring and firing of teachers.

These students were also exposed almost daily, in their neighborhoods, and outside their schools to representatives of the Nation of Islam and the Black Panther Party. Men in black suits and bowties selling *Muhammad Speaks* were a fixture of life in the city's black neighborhoods, as well as neighborhoods near schools and colleges (we had our salesman at Columbia every day). By 1969, men and women selling the Black Panther Party newspaper were almost as visible. High school students of color purchased and read these newspapers, exposing them to a critical views of American society was reinforced by neighborhood, and by school newspapers sold and distributed on the streets by white radical students and activists.

This student activism was supplemented by community organizing, some of it around the war, some of it around issues of health care and labor rights. In the fall of 1969, some activists in a then-splintered SDS decided to launch organizing projects in working-class neighborhoods in the Bronx and Queens, while the Black Panthers and Young Lords initiated remarkable campaigns to improve health care, and empower staff members and patients at the notoriously badly run and dangerous Lincoln Hospital in the South Bronx.

As a participant in one of these initiatives, the Bronx Coalition, I saw how deeply student and community activism had become embedded in what was then a largely white, but rapidly becoming multiracial section, of the Bronx. I was the only "Columbia" person in the group, which consisted of faculty in the Seek Programs (the new remediation initiative in CUNY) of Lehman and City Colleges; nurses; teachers; and postal workers' students from Lehman, Clinton, Taft, and Roosevelt High Schools, and the Bronx High School of Science; and students from SDS chapters at Lehman, Bronx Community, Fordham, and NYU. We participated in antiwar marches and demonstrations in support of imprisoned members of the Black Panther Party, but we also organized support for striking postal workers; did draft counseling for neighborhood youth; and ran a storefront women's health clinic that eventually evolved into the first abortion clinic at a New York City Hospital (Montefiore). We promoted all our activities through a community newspaper, the *Cross Bronx Express*, which we sold on the streets and outside schools for anything from a penny to a quarter, usually selling out a print run of more than three thousand papers.

We also held street rallies and concerts, picketed the local armed forces recruiting station, and tried to take our message to the youth by playing basketball in schoolyards and parks. The abortion clinic was our most lasting achievement, along with the collective accomplishment of helping to end the war. But during the two years we were together, we gave a voice to working-class people who were often left out of public discourse and whose role in building sixties protest movements has often been overlooked. One powerful example of the working-class participation in the movement to end the war took place after the invasion of Cambodia. Not only did every university in the borough go on strike but five thousand high school students, including those from Clinton and Roosevelt, marched out of school and commandeered buses and subway trains to express their outrage at this expansion of the war.

I hope this brief overview will be helpful to Occupy Wall Street as it begins to embed itself in working-class communities and to take up issues that are central to those communities' economic and social health. Certainly, the greatest victory of that period—the struggle for open admissions at City University—holds numerous lessons for current activists. But so does the role of the Harlem community and high school students in defending, protecting, and extending the Columbia strike. Now, as then, involvement of the working class is key to endowing justice movements with the energy, power, and moral stature required to extract concessions from the powerful.

SATURDAY, OCTOBER 29, 2011

The Occupy Movements and the Universities

The Occupation movements spreading around the nation and the world have the potential to revitalize university life, particularly those initiatives involving community activism and the arts. The role of arts activists in Occupy Wall Street is a story that has not been fully told. Community arts organizations in New York such as the South Bronx's Rebel Diaz Arts

Collective and Brooklyn's Global Block Collective have been involved with Occupy Wall Street for almost a month, making music videos praising the occupation, documenting the movement's growth through film, and trying to bring working-class people and people of color into the movement. The occupation has become an essential stopping point for a wide variety of performing artists, none of whom have asked for payment for their appearances (for examples, see the following videos on YouTube: "Musicians Occupy Wall Street," "Bronx Hip-Hop Duo Rebel Diaz, Live from Occupy Wall Street," "Occupy Wall St. Hip Hop Anthem: Occupation Freedom").

University faculty and participants in community outreach initiatives can only benefit from tapping into this tremendous source of energy and idealism. I have never seen students on my campus so excited about anything political or artistic as they have about these occupation movements, which have spread into outer-borough New York neighborhoods (we have "Occupy the Bronx") as well as cities throughout the nation and the world. What the movement has done is reinvigorate democratic practice—much of it face to face—widely regarded as nearly extinct among young people allegedly atomized by their cell phones and iPods. One of my students, a soccer player at Fordham, said the following about her experience on a march across the Brooklyn Bridge that led to mass arrests:

> Going to the protest I felt like this was the closest I was going to get to reliving my father/uncle's young adulthoods! While we were stuck on the bridge people were passing around cigarettes, water, food, anything anyone had they shared. Announcements were organized so everyone knew what was going on. People were yelling we're changing the world! *The world is watching*. I called my father from the bridge, told him I was getting arrested, and I could tell he was proud! It was unbelievable.

Her sense of excitement about the energy and communal spirit at OWS mirrors my own. Each time I have been at OWS I have sat in on discussion groups created on topics including Mideast politics, understanding derivatives, and educational reform. The discussions I have participated in have been rigorous, politically diverse, and to be honest, much more vibrant than most comparable discussions I have been part of at universities.

Those of us who work at universities need to find ways of connecting to a movement that has inspired so much creativity and intellectual vitality.

As someone who has been to many "Occupation" events, ranging from teach-ins, to grade-ins, to marches, and has spoken about this movement at my own university and to global media, I have experienced this energy and vitality firsthand. But most important, my *students* have experienced this and it has given them a sense that they have the power to make changes in a society that they feared had become hopelessly stagnant and hierarchical. Consider the remarks of 2010 Fordham grad Johanne Sterling, who works at Fordham's Dorothy Day Center for Service and Justice, about what participating in this movement meant to her, even though the experience got her arrested and sprayed with Mace.

> I had plans to attend a peaceful protest on Wall Street . . . I was happy to know that I was offering my voice and my support to a movement I believed in. As a young person in this country, I cannot say that I have not grown more and more unnerved with the injustices I see every day. The fact that our government is quietly but surely taking away our democratic rights (first with the Patriot Act, ironically named, and then with new voting restrictions that are being put into law), the fact that so many of my fellow graduates cannot find meaningful, rewarding work no matter how hard they try, the fact that our country's infrastructure is falling apart while the richest one percent continue to increase astronomical amounts of wealth, and the fact our justice system was able to execute and continue to execute and/or imprison innocent individuals disproportionately based on their socioeconomic position and their ethnicity, are simply a few reasons I decided to attend the rally.

This kind of civic consciousness and social justice activism is precisely what so many progressive scholars and university-based community outreach programs have sought to inspire. It is being brought to life by young people themselves in this growing national movement.

There are now more than a hundred Occupations in cities throughout the nation. They are part of a global awakening of young people that has caused governments around the world to tremble and financial elites to face the first real challenge to their power in decades.

We in the universities did not create this movement. But we ignore it at our peril. It brings to life many things we have been teaching. And it does something that we should be doing, but aren't doing enough—it empowers our students!

WEDNESDAY, OCTOBER 5, 2011

Why We Are Having a *Real* Affirmative Action Bake Sale at Fordham

The *Real* Affirmative Action Bake Sale, organized by the Affirmative Action Senior Seminar at Fordham University, not only represents my classes' outrage at the "Promote Diversity" bake sale organized by College Republicans at the University of California, Berkeley, it reflects my own frustration at the misinformation about affirmative action that prevails among large sections of the American public.

If you would believe Donald Trump—who claimed Barack Obama only got into Columbia and Harvard Law School because of affirmative action—and millions of other Americans, including many of my student's friends and relatives, you would think that preferences given minorities are the major departure from an otherwise meritocratic admissions process at the nation's top colleges.

In fact, nothing could be further from the truth. As I know from both my own research and personal experience, preferences given recruited athletes and children of alumni are far more powerful than those given underrepresented minorities and affect a far larger number of students. According to James Shulman and William Bowen, in their book *The Game of Life: College Sports and Educational Values*, recruited male athletes, in the 1999 cohort, received a 48 percent admissions advantage, as compared to 25 percent for legacies, and 18 percent for racial minorities (the comparable figures for women athletes were 54 percent, 24 percent, and 20 percent, respectively). Not only do athletes get a larger admissions advantage, Bowen and Shapiro report, they constitute a larger portion of the student population than underrepresented minorities at the nation's top colleges, averaging 20 percent at the Ivy League colleges and 40 percent at Williams, the school with the highest proportion of recruited athletes in the nation. And the vast majority of the recruited athletes at those colleges who get those admissions advantages are white, including participants in sports like men's and women's lacrosse, golf, tennis, and sailing, which few minorities participate in.

But it was not the material in *The Game of Life* that most outraged my students, it was the analysis offered in a book I used in my course for the first time, Peter Schmidt's *Color and Money: How Rich White Kids Are Winning the War Over College Affirmative Action*. According to Schmidt, higher education has become a plutocracy, where "a rich child has about twenty-five times as much chances as a poor one of someday enrolling in a college rated as highly selective or better." In the last twenty years, Schmidt claims, universities have quietly given significant admissions advantages to students whose parents can pay full tuition, make a donation to the school, or have ties to influential politicians. Schmidt's statistics, showing 74 percent of students in the top two tiers of universities come from families making over $83,000 as compared to 3 percent come from families making under $27,000 a year, enraged my students. They had no idea that students from wealthy families had such a huge advantage getting into college and when they read a September 21, 2011, *New York Times* article by Tamar Lewin, "Universities Seeking Out Students of Means," which confirmed all of Schmidt's conclusions, they got even angrier.

Enter the College Republicans' "Increase Diversity" Bake Sale at Berkeley, which charged whites, Asians, and males higher prices than blacks, Latinos and women, and left athletes, legacies, and children of the wealthy out of the equation. When I suggested that we might consider organizing a bake sale whose categories and pricing structure were based on the materials we had been covering in class, they jumped all over the idea. They formed committees to write press releases, secure the support of campus organizations, develop a price structure consistent with what really goes on in college admissions, and make sure we have an ample supply of baked goods. Thanks to all their hard work, the sale will take place Friday, October 7, from 11 a.m. to 3 p.m., in Fordham's McGinley Student Center, and use the following price structure, based on the latest research on actual advantages in college admissions:

Women (General Admission) $1.30

Men (General Admission) $1.25

Underrepresented Minorities $1.00

Legacies (Children of Alumni) $1.00

Recruited Athletes $0.50

Children of the Very Wealthy $0.25

We are also calling on students in other universities to follow our example and organize bakes sales of their own based on sound research, not rumors and myths. The goal is not only to dramatize the extraordinary power of great wealth in American society—something highlighted by the Wall Street Occupation and the protests inspired by it around the country—but to remove the stigma that has been placed on minority students as recipients of unfair preferences. These students are tired of being attacked as an affront to American "meritocracy." Enough is enough!

My students are excited and confident, looking forward to the discussion and debate on and off campus their bake sale will inspire. I am very proud of the courage and energy they have displayed in organizing this groundbreaking event!

WEDNESDAY, AUGUST 10, 2011

The Basis of My Current Optimism about Youth Activism

A lot of people I respect have been extremely skeptical about my prediction that we are seeing, in its early stages, a new wave of youth activism. They think I am being a starry-eyed optimist based on my limited contacts in liberal New York, especially in the Bronx.

But based on the same kind of contacts, in the same place, in the middle and late 1970s, I predicted, correctly as it turned out, a long period of conservative hegemony in American politics, with young people leading the way. Let me explain how I came to that conclusion before moving back to the current situation.

The early and middle '70s were a rough time in New York City, in the Bronx in particular. We suffered deindustrialization and disinvestment, a heroin epidemic, rising crime rates, white and middle-class flight, and finally a fiscal crisis and bank takeover of city government that decimated education, recreational, and youth services. I experienced all these things, directly and indirectly, and also watched large sections of the Bronx burn as I took the Third Avenue El and the 4 train from my apartment in Manhattan to my new job at Fordham.

But what made me most pessimistic was not all of these real-life tragedies, it was the attitude of my students at Fordham. By 1975 and 1976, the vast majority of my white students at Fordham had come to look at any form of idealism and social consciousness as a luxury they couldn't afford (my Black and Latino students, whose numbers were shrinking, still shared many of my views). They looked on me as comical and pathetic, a '60s relic who still thought that the pursuit of justice and equality was a realistic life goal. Their strategy was clear. They were going to survive, and if possible prosper, by keeping as far away from the problems of the inner city as they could, and not waste any energy on causes that had no chance of succeeding. Whereas my first students and Fordham in 1970–71 were comrades in struggle who shared my dreams of a better world, these young people were going to make sure that they were untouched by the tragedies that surrounded them.

The attitudes I encountered then lasted for at least ten years, not receding until the late 1980s. It led me to withdraw much of my energy from teaching and put it into research, physical fitness (I won seven straight Brooklyn public parks tennis championships in the late '70s/early '80s), and bringing up my children as competitive athletes. I continued to work with students who were justice activists, but they were few and far between. Virtually all of the people I worked with in community organizations were '60s veterans.

Now fast forward to the present. My classes at Fordham are packed with students who are committed to justice work, and who do wonderful community service projects in the Bronx and all over the globe. More and more of these students are becoming radicalized by the inequalities that surround them and are thinking of ways they can make an impact through the work they do. Many have gone to work for nonprofits, some have gone into the Jesuit Volunteer Corps and the Peace Corps, some have helped found innovative social justice organizations in New York City, such as Momma's Hip Hop Kitchen, the Rebel Diaz Arts Collective, and The Space at Tompkins. More than a few have decided to enter teaching as a career, some through graduate programs, some through alternate certification programs like the New York City Teaching Fellows and Teach for America.

Equally important, ever since I began writing and speaking in defense of public school teachers, and challenging the testing/privatization model dominating mainstream education discourse, I have been literally deluged with emails from young teachers, in New York and around the country, fighting the same battles, some of them looking for support, some of them looking to connect with existing networks, some of them launching remarkable initiatives on their own. These emails have only accelerated since the Save Our Schools Conference and March, convincing me that event was only going to increase the level of organizing among teachers around the nation, especially among those new to the profession.

So while the political situation in the nation today is at least as grim as it was in the middle and late 70s it *feels* different to me because I am surrounded by young people who feel the same way about the injustices of this society that I do, and what's more, are willing to do something about those problems.

Their energy and their passion give me hope.

TUESDAY, JUNE 28, 2011

Test-Driven School Reform— a Brilliant Strategy to Make Working-Class Youth Disengage from School

If I were going to figure out a plan to get working-class youth to disengage from school, these would be my major components. First, I would make students sit at their desks all day and force them to constantly memorize materials to prepare for tests. Second, I would take away recess and eliminate gym. Third, I would cut out arts projects and hands-on science experiments. Fourth, I would limit the number of school trips. Fifth, I would take away extracurricular activities like band, dance teams, and talent shows and reduce the number of athletic teams, so that students' energies could be exclusively concentrated on strictly academic tasks.

But wait a minute, isn't that exactly what the dominant education reform movement in the United States is doing, from Secretary of Education Arne Duncan on down? Aren't policy makers forcing schools to add more and more standardized tests and threatening teachers and principals with mass firings if their scores on those tests don't go up, with the result that anything that isn't test driven is eliminated from the school culture?

Yes, that's what's going on in education, all across the country. Starting with No Child Left Behind and continuing through Race to the Top, we have been hell bent on making students from working-class and poor families economically competitive with their wealthier peers by increasing their test scores and improving their graduation rates. And the way to do that, we believe, is to make them devote more and more of their time to acquiring basic literacy, and then translating those skills into passing standardized tests in every subject.

But in formulating this strategy, which from the outside appears to be sensible and rational, we erase the worldview of the very students in whose interests we claim to be acting. We treat working-class students as passive recipients of a service who will do whatever we tell them to, rather than critical thinkers and impassioned (if sometimes impulsive) historical actors, who respond to school policies based on their culture, values, and their sense of how those policies affect their short-term and long-term interests.

As someone who grew up in a tough working-class neighborhood, and has worked in similar neighborhoods as a coach, community organizer, and teacher, I can assure you that young people in these communities are anything but passive when it comes to responding to externally imposed authority. Although some children in those communities accept authority unquestioningly, many more make it a matter of pride to challenge and test adults outside their families who claim power over them, and they get respect from their peers for doing so. No teacher, coach, or social worker assigned to teach "in the hood" gets a free pass from that testing, which sometimes reaches the proportions of hazing. Whatever respect you get has to be earned.

And what goes for teachers or community workers goes for schools. Most people in poor and working-class neighborhoods do not see schools as working in their or their children's interests. Their own experiences with schools have often not been that positive, and their attitudes of skepticism and even hostility readily transfer to their children. Overcoming that ingrained skepticism not only requires efforts by individual teachers, it requires efforts by entire schools to make students feel that they are places where they are respected, where their voice can be heard and their culture validated, and where they can actually have some fun. The best inner city schools I know not only make sure they maintain a welcoming atmosphere, but try to create a festive one, with music and the arts being part of every public meeting, sports events highlighted, and where student, parent, and community input is incorporated into every dimension of the school culture.

Now enter the Era of Test Mania, with administrators and teachers panicked they will lose their jobs if they do not produce continuous positive results on one high-stakes test after another. Forget the school being a place where student and community creativity can be validated. Every bit of time, energy, and emotion must be devoted to test prep. Students have to sit still and listen, memorize, and regurgitate large bodies of information. Time for self-expression disappears. Time for physical activity is erased. The school becomes a place filled with stress and fear.

Some students will conform, and may even pass all the tests that they are given, but just as many—a good portion of them boys—will rebel, either by disrupting classes, challenging the teacher vandalizing the school, or not going to school altogether. There is no way that working-class kids like me or a lot of the kids that I coached and taught over the years are going to sit in school and obediently memorize material if you don't give them some physical outlets, a chance to move and express themselves, and opportunities to speak out on issues important to them. When you are brought up to "take no sh-t from anyone" and stand up for yourself, you are not about to allow teachers and school administrators to humiliate you, intimidate you, and silence your rebellious spirit. In neighborhoods where respect of peers is the key to survival, the underground economy beckons, and many people, in the words of Big Pun "would rather sell reefer than do pizza delivery," schools that try to discipline students rather than engage them will find they are in for trouble.

The vision of school reform currently dominant in our country, where teachers and principals browbeat and harass students to pass tests in order to keep themselves from being fired, is going to blow up in our face. And while teacher protest will be an important component of the resistance, it will be student disengagement and violence that will ultimately put this phase of reform to rest.

TUESDAY, MAY 10, 2011

From Centers of Obedience to Centers of Resistance: A Strategy to Restore Hope to the City's Public Schools

A tragic series of events is unfolding in working-class New York. The lingering effects of the recession, irresponsible private investments, and federal and state budget cuts, coupled with a failure to raise taxes on the wealthy, have created a toxic brew that is eroding the already-fragile living standards of the city's poor and creating higher levels of homelessness, hunger, and violence.

Nowhere is this more visible than in the housing market where a combination of foreclosures on private homes; failed investments by private equity companies; the phasing out of federal rent subsidies; the proposed end of the Work Advantage Program in New York State; and rising rents in public housing have taken thousands of units of affordable housing out of commission, and forced tens of thousands of people to "double" and "triple up" with friends and relatives, or move into shelters.

The effects of this are visible throughout the city's public schools where more and more children are arriving at school stressed, hungry, and frightened as their families are displaced and their ability to assure their children of adequate sleep, food, and study space is undermined. Once, such wounded children could find safe, protected space in libraries and after-school programs, but with upcoming budget cuts to libraries (which will cut public library hours from forty to twenty-eight a week) and to after-school and recreational programs, these youngsters will be increasingly on their own, and forced to spend time in public places—streets, subways, and shelters—where danger lurks for young people without adult supervision and protection. In the face of this unfolding tragedy, what are teachers, principals, and school guidance counselors to do?

The official policy of the NYC Department of Education is to pretend this isn't happening. Their response is more assessments, more tests, more ratings, more pressure on students and everyone who is working with them. And the result is predictable. The misery of the students is spreading to the teachers whose spirits are being broken, not only by the violent incidents occurring in schools with increasing frequency, but by the evident pain their students are in. It is visible in their inability to concentrate in class, and their harrowing stories of hunger and homelessness and family catastrophe. All of this is taking place, I must add, amidst fierce pressure from the DOE to raise test scores and graduation rates, with the fear of school closings and loss of employment as potential penalties.

It's time to flip the script. Schools must become places where students in trouble are protected and nurtured, and where the adults working there fight for them as if they were their own children.

Every New York City public school should become a center of resistance to budget cuts, not only in schools but in libraries, after-school centers, and programs that provide or protect affordable housing. The culture of compliance and obedience, which has left teachers and students alike demoralized and terrorized, must be replaced by a culture of resistance. The school must become a place where political education and political organizing takes place and unites teachers, parents, and students in strategies, not seen since the '60s, that will put pressure on elected officials. Pressure to restore housing subsidies, expand funding for after-school programs, restore library budgets to their 2008 levels, bring more arts and sports programs into the public schools, create more school health centers, end all teacher layoffs, and tax the wealthy to pay for these reforms.

Not only will such actions restore a sense of agency to teachers who are regularly vilified in the press and by public officials as the cause of students "failures," it will give hope and inspiration to tens of thousands of young people and members of their families who are afraid that their lives will involve anything other than hardship and pain.

It's time to transform New York City public schools from centers of fear and intimidation to "liberated zones," where teachers, students, and parents can talk freely about how to make their schools and neighborhoods provide hope and opportunity to their children. And if that leads them directly to the steps of City Hall, the State Legislature, the US Congress, or the headquarters of Wall Street banks, so be it.

On a small scale, this is starting to happen. A group of insurgent teachers and parents have started a program called "Fight Back Fridays" with actions taking place at public schools around the city on May 20. But this should only be the beginning of a mighty wave of protest that will transform the New York City public schools from centers of obedience into centers of resistance to the budget cuts and to government by the rich, for the rich, which seems to be the trend, not only in New York but around the country.

The sleeping giant is starting to awake. Students, teachers, and parents, joined together, can be a mighty force for justice and democracy.

SUNDAY, DECEMBER 16, 2012

The Power of Kindness: Personal Reflections on Young Men and Violence

During my forty-plus years as a teacher, coach, and community organizer, I have spent a good portion of my time dealing with angry, wounded young men, often on a one-to-one basis. When I was coaching, I always took the boys that no one else could handle. People having difficulty with their sons sometimes send them to spend a day with me at Fordham, and faculty and administrators occasionally ask me to mentor students, mostly men, who are having difficulty adjusting to the school.

I work well with such young people because I was once one of them. Although I was judged academically gifted, I grew up angry and violent. My parents hit me on a regular basis because they thought it was their only way of controlling me, and from elementary school through high school, I got in fights on a regular basis in and out of school. Eventually I was forced to transfer from one high school to another out of my district. In college, I physically threatened roommates, and when I got involved in SDS in my graduate school years, I was given responsibility for beating up right-wing students trying to stop our protests, and worked the front lines in conflicts with police.

As I settled into adulthood, I was exposed and had my actions critiqued by radical feminists, and I got involved in love relationships with strong women. I began to come to grips with my anger, and prevent it from poisoning the lives of those around me. I learned to anticipate and contain my rage, but I also learned something about its sources, including an absence of kindness and compassion on the part of my parents, who felt relentless pressure was the best way to spur achievement, and hard discipline the best way to stem rebellion.

As I got involved in teaching and began coaching, I started applying what I had learned to young men who reminded me of myself. Some of what eased the way to building a connection was my body language and affect, which allowed them to recognize a kindred spirit. But some of it was something I would tell them, which was that no matter how outrageous they got, I would not give up on them. They could come and hang out with me no questions asked, any time, get something to eat, listen to music, watch television (if they were in my neighborhood) and not say a word if they weren't ready to. If they were ready to open up, we could talk about anything they wanted. The other thing was physical contact, which ranged from high fives, elaborate soul handshakes, and hugs, I put my arm around them when they were angry. I wanted to give them the sense that when they were with me they were protected, cared for, and safe. Even though we never used the word, I wanted them to know they were loved.

It's not that I didn't think these troubled young men needed discipline. As a coach, or a teacher in the classroom, I exposed them to plenty of that. It's that on a one-on-one basis, what they most needed was kindness and space to be themselves without worrying that they would be discarded if they acted out. They were allowed to make mistakes without worrying about me running away. And guess what? That very knowledge calmed them down.

I am not saying that I was a miracle worker or master psychologist. I was a caring adult lucky enough to pursue a career as a teacher, and I never forgot the wounded child inside me. I reached out to other wounded children to give them confidence that they could eventually overcome their pain.

So here's my thought: We need to have more people do this kind of thing to the wounded children that surround us, inside and outside of our schools. If we discard them, punish them, drug them, and put them behind walls, both real and invisible, their rage will return to haunt us. If we embrace them, care for them, and give them space to grow and make mistakes, some of them will find their way to happiness and security.

TUESDAY, OCTOBER 16, 2012

Today, They Drug Boys Like Me

When I read the *New York Times* article about the psychiatrist in a poor county in Georgia who was drugging kids who do not have ADHD to help them do well in school, I thought, "There but for the grace of God go I. I was lucky I was born in 1946 not 1996. They would definitely try to drug a kid like me in a growing number of America's public schools."

I was the kind of kid who drove teachers and parents crazy. I was a good student and a good test taker, so much so that I ended up skipping two grades and was constantly made fun of by other kids in my tough Brooklyn neighborhood. But I was disrespectful to teachers, and always getting in fights with other kids, inside and outside of class. My teachers complained to my parents, and my parents constantly threatened to send me to yeshiva or military school, but somehow the schools I went to managed to cope with me and other kids like me, most of them boys, without drugs or expulstions because they knew how to tire us out and challenge us with physical activities. They also assigned us responsibilities that today only adults are allowed to accept.

Take physical activity. In elementary school, we had free play before school and during lunchtime when we played punch ball, kickball, and tag, running ourselves into exhaustion. We also had gym every day. But that wasn't all. My elementary school was open from three to five and seven to nine every day of the week for supervised activity. I used it regularly to play basketball and knock hockey. When you combined all these activities, it was not unusual for me to be engaged in physical activity, in and after school, two to three hours a day. Not only did this tire me out, making it much easier to sit still and concentrate on lessons, it gave me something to look forward to other than harassing teachers and fighting. I still got in trouble, but only a fraction of the trouble I would have gotten in if I didn't have all that physical activity.

When I got to fifth grade, my teacher assigned me to two important student-run activities: the audiovisual squad, whose responsibility was to show movies in all the classes; and the Safety Patrol, who helped younger students cross the street. Both of these activities were given to some of the toughest kids in the school, and without exception, they rose to the occasion and did their jobs with great responsibility and pride. Today, these responsibilities are paid positions given to school aides and paraprofessionals, but in those years, they helped young people whose leadership skills were often directed negatively and turned them into positive figures in the school community. They certainly helped me.

In junior high, the same dynamic prevailed. Not only did we have gym every day and play games in the schoolyard before school and during lunch hour, but we started to have a whole range of organized activities that gave students an outlet for their talents, ranging from a theater program and school teams to a band and an orchestra. And though the junior high school was not convenient to go to for after-school activity because it was out of my neighborhood, I could still play basketball in my elementary school night center, which was right around the corner from my house. Once again, I was engaged in physical activity at least two hours a day, not including the time I spent playing in the school band.

In New York City today, and a growing number of public schools around the country, the activities that kept me on course have been eliminated or drastically curtailed, either because of budget cuts, professionalization of what were once student responsibilities, or pressures to raise scores on standardized tests. I cannot think of one public school in New York City that offers its students two to three hours of physical activity a day; most students are lucky if they get thirty minutes. Few schools below the level of high schools have school teams, bands, and orchestras; even less have after-school programs both in the afternoon and evening.

So what happens to restless, rebellious students from tough neighborhoods, especially boys? Are they given activities that allow them to use their physical energy constructively? Are they given responsibilities that allow them to be positive leaders or make use of their athletic or artistic talents? Increasingly, the answer is no. They are asked to sit still at their desks hour after hour and try to absorb information that often has no visible relevance to their lives and nothing to spark their interests. And if they rebel and act out, as many of them will be prone to do, or fail to concentrate on preparing for tests? They not only are jeopardizing their own academic futures, they may be threatening the jobs of their teachers, principals, and the fate of their entire school.

Given how high the "stakes" are on getting them to perform or conform, two options seem irresistible to teachers and administrators. Getting them to leave the school, which is not always easy, or giving them behavior-modifying drugs, which is becoming increasingly prevalent. To me, this is a perversion of education and of the health professions. It is a cruel, cynical shortcut to producing conformity to a system that is undermining the health of the children trapped in it. I think of the how many children like me there are in Georgia and Texas and Nebraska and California and New York who will never have a chance to realize that the power and energy that lies within them can transform the world around them, because they are being drugged into submission. This is personal to me. And I will expose it and challenge it with every weapon at my command.

WEDNESDAY, APRIL 4, 2012

Making Play Disappear—What Test-Based School Reform and the Suppression of the Occupy Movement Have in Common

One of the most threatening features of the Occupy movement was its playfulness and spontaneity. The beating of the drums; the impromptu marches through city streets; the group discussions that could break out at any moment; the musicians of all types who would come to perform and whose performance was immediately captured and disseminated online. All of these elements created a festive atmosphere that grabbed the imagination of people around the country and helped the movement spread like wildfire. It is this playful and defiant spirit, made possible by the possession of communal spaces in the centers of towns and cities, that mayors and police departments seemed to find especially threatening because it challenged the order and obedience that they saw as essential to the smooth running of their cities and the maintenance of vibrant economies. Evicting the Occupy camps, something partially coordinated by Homeland Security, removed the threat of a contagion of freedom and spontaneity in their midst.

The same obsession with order and obedience is dominant in the educational policies being promoted by leaders of both political parties, and coordinated by the US Department of Education. Everywhere around the country, schools are eliminating arts, music, and gym—and in the lower grades, play and recess—to make time for more standardized tests. Increasingly, school time, from kindergarten and pre-K on, is being transformed into preparation for standardized tests, with the results of those tests guiding the futures of students, teachers, administrators, and at times whole schools. Not only is playtime being eliminated, but activities that leave room for imagination and creativity are also being squeezed out of the curriculum in one subject area after another. Dreamers and those who express themselves through physical activity find their talents devalued.

Those who are uncomfortable sitting still, and who, through no fault of their own, have difficulty absorbing information in the rigid forms that schools increasingly present it, are marginalized and humiliated.

Increasingly, we now live in a nation that is declaring war on play. Perhaps this is necessary to manage a society where upward mobility is no longer possible for a large portion of our citizens, and where the fate of most people will be performing low-paid work under strict surveillance. It is certainly convenient for sustaining the rule of the one percent.

But let us be very clear. In suppressing playfulness and spontaneity, we undermine the parts of ourselves that make us the most human, most compassionate, and most capable of adapting to new circumstances. And we fatally weaken whatever vestiges of freedom and democracy left in our social order.

THURSDAY, MARCH 21, 2013

A Day at Sheepshead Bay: Where Young People Prove More Special Than Their Needs

I just got through an incredible experience at Sheepshead Bay High School in Brooklyn where I was invited to talk about the history of hip-hop to two classes of special needs students, one led by my wonderful former student Anne Brewka. The day began with passing through a scanner and a metal detector, which I always set off because of my artificial hip. Then Anne met me, and gave me a heads up on the group I would be talking to. Many of the young people in the group in the two classes were physically disabled, some less so than others, and twelve of the twenty plus in the group had their own paraprofessionals, some because they were in wheelchairs and others because of behavioral issues.

What happened perfectly embodied the principle "never judge a book by its cover," and even more so the principle "every child has magnificent gifts to offer the world." In the course of a ninety-plus-minute presentation where I lectured, asked questions, played music, and rapped, the students in the class turned what began as a lecture into an old-school hip-hop party. Students rapped, danced, created complex rhythms on their desks and on the floor, and asked great questions. Freed from some of the restraints and discipline more "socialized" students display, these young people let loose with an explosion of talent and of joyous creativity that blew everyone in the room away, even the paras, who started the day somewhat dour and then clapped their hands with the beat and cheered their students on. The teachers just let the party go on. It reached its high point when I put on Afrika Bambaattaa's "Looking for a Perfect Beat," and a seven-minute b-boy/b-girl battle began.

I have had great experiences speaking to high school groups where people danced, rapped, and beatboxed. But nothing like this. Nothing like brilliant questions coming from a young man in a wheelchair who understood the essence of what hip-hop lyricism can mean to disfranchised young people who are routinely treated with contempt. Or three young men in a special needs class creating beats on a desk for another one of their peers who rapped brilliantly. Or two young men trading b-boy moves that would have gotten them dollar tips on the subway.

This is education. This is what should happen in our schools. Every day. It is art that unlocks the key to the mind and the soul. Not for some students. For all of them.

SATURDAY, MARCH 2, 2013

What the Bronx Lost When the Rebel Diaz Arts Collective Was Evicted

Three weeks ago, I was asked by a superb young elementary school teacher with a long history of doing multimedia arts projects with her students if I could find someone to work with her on a soundtrack she was creating for a student presentation on gun violence in America. She had the lyrics and the choreography set, and she just needed someone to create the beats, then have the students sing over them. After thinking long and hard, I directed her to DJ Charlie Hustle, one of the top DJs in the Rebel Diaz Arts Collective (RDACBX), and also one of my former students. Charlie responded enthusiastically, and last week she took her students down to the Arts Collective Studios, where they spend several hours recording the track. Nothing was charged for the beat making or the studio time. This was donated as a community service by RDACBX, which is committed to giving Bronx youth access to first-rate studio equipment while teaching them the technical expertise to create music with it. Less than a week after these students recorded their track, marshals and the NYPD smashed down the door of the Rebel Diaz Arts Collective, removed the people living and working there, threw much of its equipment into the street, and put new locks on the doors. In the process, its state-of-the-art recording studio was totally destroyed. This was done at the break of dawn, with no prior warning. Did local elected officials know about this? Did they approve the action? At this point no one knows, but one thing is clear. A precious resource to the youth of the Bronx, one that provided an outlet for artistic expression and taught them the technical skills that underlay the producing and preservation of art, was destroyed.

That this took place in an arts-starved community, with only a small number of arts programs in the local schools. There are no after-school programs or night centers with the access to state-of-the-art recording equipment and performance opportunities offered by the Rebel Diaz Arts Collective. This makes the indifference of local officials to this eviction near criminal.

In coming months, the burden will fall on the elected leaders of the Bronx, from the borough president on down, to find alternate space for the Rebel Diaz Arts Collective. They will also need to give them funding for their destroyed equipment, so that they can once again provide the gift of artistic expression to Bronx youth, and empower the teachers and community organizers who work with them.

From the mambo and jazz era of the '40s through the rise of doo-wop, funk, and salsa in the '50s and '60s, to the dawn of hip-hop in the '70s and '80s, to the hip life and bachata of today brought by the Bronx's new immigrants, the arts have been the lifeblood of Bronx neighborhoods, and a particular inspiration to Bronx youth. The Rebel Diaz Arts Collective, which keeps that tradition alive, deserves the full support of everyone who loves the Bronx and believes in its future.

SUNDAY, MARCH 24, 2013

Chicago School Closings and the Murder of Kimani Gray— the Atrophied Conscience of Apartheid America

Little by little, we have created an apartheid nation—a place where profound spatial and moral divisions separate the lives of the privileged and the unfortunate. The boundaries are not strictly racial, though those on the lower side of the divide are overwhelmingly people of color. Nor are they marked by gates, walls, and fences. Rather, they are enforced by a complex set of codes followed by law enforcement authorities who have acquired immense power to assure public safety, since the imposition of the war on drugs and the war on terror. Those powers that have effectively stopped the poor from doing anything to prevent their marginalization and immiseration, and which have given wealthy elites virtually immunity from political action, mass protest, or street crime.

You can see this in New York City if you shop in a newly wealthy neighborhood, like Park Slope, go to an arts destination in Manhattan, or go to one of the boroughs' great universities, like Columbia, NYU, or Fordham. Groups of young people from one of the outer boroughs' poor neighborhoods are often congregating in groups. But police practices have made it clear that they are not welcome there—that their very presence constitutes a virtual threat, a "crime waiting to happen." But youth of color cleansing and spatial controls are not just imposed in already established centers of wealth. In Bedford-Stuyvesant and Red Hook, both gentrifying areas, police practices keep young people penned into neighborhood housing projects, and wary of walking streets in a group where middle-class residents have moved or hip cafes have opened. Very quickly, young people with certain race and class markers learn that they are subject to being stopped, questioned, and frisked in almost all spaces out of their neighborhoods, and in a growing number of spaces where they actually live.

But worse yet, daily life for young people of color who are poor is out of sight and out of mind, and thereby unimaginable by middle-class and wealthy residents of cities, and the mayors of those cities. Because they never talk to young people who are on the receiving end of these spatial controls and never see those controls in action, they can pretend they don't exist. Their consciences have atrophied when it comes to the fundamental realities of life for the young and the poor.

Two recent events dramatize this for me: the police murder of Kimani Gray in East Flatbush, Brooklyn, and the school closing order given by Mayor Rahm Emanuel in Chicago. New York's mayor Michael Bloomberg has never reached out to the grieving mother of a sixteen-year-old boy who was killed for doing nothing more than walking home from a neighborhood party. Instead, he hides behind a "narrative of criminality" used to hide the ugly facts of Kimani Gray's death, and pretends his death was an outgrowth of a "stop and frisk" procedure initiated by plain clothes police, this will *never* happen to young people in the mayor's family or social circle. Kimani Gray became one of New York City's legion of "disposable youth" who must be policed and contained in each aspect of their lives to make the city's engines of economic growth secure. He could be snuffed out without anyone in power losing a moment of sleep.

Similarly tens of thousands of young people of color whose lives will be disrupted by the school closings ordered by Mayor Rahm Emanuel in Chicago could be conveniently erased from his thoughts by a ski trip because his own children (and their friends), safely enrolled in the University of Chicago Lab School, would never experience the disruptions. The impact of these policies would be felt by "Other People's Children"—the same people who live in fear of gun violence, gang violence, police containment, and feel alternately penned into poor neighborhoods, or pushed out of the city altogether.

A leadership that can inflict this kind of containment and moral erasure on a large portion of their city's population can only be described as pro-

foundly corrupt, but we are all complicit insofar as we have allowed our
security to be built on edifices of other people's suffering.

FRIDAY, APRIL 26, 2013

It Takes a Child to Lead a Village— Thank You to the Test Refusers of New York State

At the dawn of the last day of the weeks of testing in New York State, I want
to offer my sincere thanks and deepest gratitude to the thousands of children and their families who participated in the largest collective act of test
refusal in American history. At a time when high-stakes testing is deforming
public education in virtually every state in the nation, when it has assumed
the character of an out-of-control train that no one seems able or willing
to stop, you have shown that people of courage and character can lead us
away from a path that will only end in tragedy.

What you have done has not been easy. You have been vilified, ostra-
cized, threatened, and in some instances punished in ways that no children
of any age should have to endure. You have been forced to sit in silence for
hours staring ahead, excluded from extracurricular activities, and told you
will be denied promotion to the next grade, or access to honors programs.
A few of you have been told you are jeopardizing your teachers' jobs, your
schools funding, or real estate prices in your town. More than a few have
been told that your actions will make it difficult to get into a good college.

But as in other great movements when people take risks based upon
deeply held convictions, this campaign of intimidation has backfired. For
the first time since the opt-out movement has started, civil liberties lawyers
have stepped forward to defend opting-out children and families, and a
lawsuit has been filed in Rochester against one such family subject to particularly grievous abuses.

And the courage you have displayed in the face of this has also brought
unprecedented publicity to the opt-out movement. Literally scores of articles,

TV stories, local media pieces and major pieces in the *New York Times* and other national publications have run. Every politician and editorial writer in the state, and probably most around the nation, now know that thousands of New Yorkers have said no to uncontrolled testing, and some are starting to express doubts about the current directions of education policy in the nation.

Because of this, everyone who cares about the future of public education in the country is in your debt for showing us that resistance to current education reform policies is both possible and necessary.

You have shown us that while "It Takes a Village to Raise a Child" sometimes "It Takes a Child to Lead a Village."

Part 3:

Lessons of Bronx Schools

Sometimes Superman—and Lois Lane—Live Next Door: What We Can Learn about Teaching from the Pruitts of East 168th Street

Today I had a chance to spend time with two members of the most amazing family of educators I know, the Pruitts of East 168th Street in the Morrisania section of the Bronx. The Pruitt family, which moved into a small row house on 168th Street in the early 1940s when the neighborhood was mostly Jewish, had five children, all of whom became teachers. Harriet (McFeeters) worked more than forty years in the Bronx as a teacher, principal, and assistant district superintendent; James, taught social studies in Bronx high schools along with a stint running the Upward Bound program at Fordham; Bess, was a gym and dance instructor at Evander Childs High School and founded one of the first dance promotion companies run by a black woman; and Henry and Janet were teachers and school administrators in Englewood and Newark, New Jersey, respectively.

At a time when improving our public schools, especially in poor and working-class communities, has become a national obsession, it is astonishing to me that no one in the New York City Department of Education has sought to draw upon the experiences of this family for clues on how to recruit and retain talented teachers. Every one of these remarkable individuals spent their entire professional life as teachers and school administrators, and achieved remarkable success in inspiring students and teachers who worked with them.

But the idea of recruiting lifetime educators seems to have low priority for those guiding America's school systems. Teach for America (TFA), the largest and most prestigious alternate certification program in the nation, actually promotes teaching in poverty schools as a pathway for entering more prestigious careers (TFA once put up a poster at Fordham explaining how joining TFA could improve one's chances of getting into Stanford Business School!) It keeps only a fraction of its recruits in the classroom for more than five years. Under the Bloomberg/Klein regime in New York, the Department of Education has made a concerted effort to replace veteran teachers with newcomers from alternative certification programs, many of whom burn out and leave in two or three years. Recruiting people who grew up in working-class neighborhoods and giving them first-class training so they can return as teachers to the neighborhoods they grew up in doesn't fit the business models dominating educational policy, which rely on maximum flexibility and mobility of the educational workforce.

However, when it comes to teaching, flexibility and mobility may not be the traits we need. The best teachers do more than impart skills and subject matter to their students; they build relationships that last lifetimes. I have seen this firsthand with the two members of the Pruitt family I know best, Jim Pruitt and Harriet McFeeters.

You cannot go anywhere in the Bronx with these two individuals without running into someone who was one of their students or colleagues. Invariably, there are hugs, kisses, and comments to me about how the person I was with either changed his or her life (if he/she was a student) or helped them do their job better (if he/she was a teacher or principal). But my evidence for this is not just based on individual encounters. I had the privilege of attending the retirement party for Jim Pruitt that brought together more than two hundred people, most of whom were his former students from Morris and Kennedy High Schools. I also, almost every year, drop in on the Fordham Upward Bound reunion, where more than fifty black and Latino men who grew up in the Bronx reminisce about the experiences they had under Jim Pruitt's mentorship.

There are a few things about the Pruitt family history that might provide clues to their success. They grew up in an African American, working-class family and learning and public service were held up as ideals no matter the wealth one possessed. Each child attended New York City public schools, and attended New York public universities. And two members of the family, Bess and Harriet, lived in the family house in Morrisania during all the years they worked in the Bronx public schools. They were there during years that included an arson and abandonment cycle that decimated many portions of their neighborhood; as a fiscal crisis took music, arts, and after-school programs out of the public schools; and a crack epidemic destroyed many young people and their families. Through all this, Bess and Harriet remained in their neighborhood and remained in Bronx schools, guiding young people whom others gave up on, and mentoring new teachers who came in to work for them.

If you are looking for superheroes, educators whose experience may hold the key to helping young people growing up in poverty embrace education, the best place to look may not be in the charter schools of Harlem, but in a little row house on East 168th Street between Prospect and Union Avenues in the Morrisania section of the Bronx. I know that's where I go, along with a great public school in the Bronx, PS 140 (headed by a remarkable principal, Paul Cannon, who grew up only two blocks away from the Pruitts), when I'm looking for inspiration.

Maybe someday, when the people running our schools stop looking to Wall Street or Hearst Publications for guidance, they will turn to the people who have a proven track record for educating inner-city youth, and who did it—and are doing it—in the neighborhoods they grew up in.

SATURDAY, SEPTEMBER 26, 2009

A Visit to PS 140: How an Extraordinary School Used *The Rat That Got Away* to Promote Literacy and Professional Development

On Friday morning, September 25, Allen Jones, author of *The Rat That Got Away: A Bronx Memoir*, joined me for a visit to PS 140, a Bronx school I have worked with for the last four years. A group of teachers wanted to meet with us to discuss the book.

For Allen and me, the visit was a profoundly moving experience. First of all, to see a group of twenty teachers gathered for a book group at 7:30 a.m. on a Friday morning, each of whom had read the book cover to cover, said something very powerful about the culture of PS 140 and the appeal of *The Rat That Got Away*. In a school where the principal is often in the building seven days a week, teachers think nothing of being in the building early in the morning or late into the night to enhance their own professional development, or do something that might benefit their students or the larger school community. Allen and I looked at the faces of the teachers assembled, mostly women, mostly (but not all) black and Latino. Clearly, from their affect and conversation, these were people who had grown up in the city, and we felt a twinge of anxiety along with the excitement. Would they like the book? Would the find it true to life? Would they feel it captured their experience and the experience of the young people they worked with every day?

After I gave a brief introduction thanking the teachers for coming and explained how the book was written, I asked the teachers what they thought of the book, and urged them to be completely honest and not worry if what they said offended us. What followed left us humbled, gratified, and deeply moved. The first teacher to speak, Mary Dixon Lake, herself a published poet and children's book author, said the book brought to life the world of her childhood in Bedford-Stuyvesant, and that Allen's portrait of his father captured the aura of power and respect that surrounded her own father and many black fathers she grew up around. Another teacher, Pam Lewis, said that even though she grew up in another Bronx housing project (Edenwald instead of Patterson) twenty-five years later than Allen, his description of the sights, sounds, and smells of the project grounds when he went to church at eight on a Sunday morning was exactly how she remembers her trips to church during her own childhood. Another teacher came forward to praise the book's language, saying that she appreciated how well Allen captured the way people in the street spoke, it was the first book about the Bronx and that where the language of the main characters was wholly believable and authentic.

But the most powerful moment came when Mike Napolitano, a teacher in the school who had grown up in the Patterson Houses, and whose older brothers knew and played ball with Allen said, "That was me! That was us." Echoing Allen, he described project halls so clean that he could get on his hands and knees and push model cars through them, and people who trusted their neighbors so much that they left their doors open all day. People of all races and ethnicities were in and out of each others' apartments, eating one another's food, listening to one another's music, and building friendships that crossed racial lines. He went on to praise Allen for giving recognition to all the coaches and community center directors who worked with neighborhood youth, saying, "I played for them too." He laughingly affirmed the accuracy of Allen's depiction of the stores where hustlers and wannabee hustlers bought their clothes, pulling out a photograph of one of his older brothers in a Bly shop shirt! As Mike spoke and and Allen nodded in mutual appreciation of their shared experience, his fellow teachers looked at Mike with new eyes and new respect, as they realized that the stories he had always been telling everyone about life in "the Patterson," even though he was an Italian American in his mid-forties, were all true! By the end of the discussion, he and Allen were hugging each other like long-lost brothers, trading phone numbers, and making arrangements to visit a ninety-seven-year-old basketball mentor named Mr. Page who still alive, lucid, and residing on the Grand Concourse.

After the book group ended, with hugs and photos and promises by Allen to return to the school, Principal Cannon took us up to Mike Napolitano's classroom, where he was using *The Rat That Got Away* to promote literacy, reading skills, and an understanding of local history in his class of fourth-grade boys. The class was part of Principal Cannon's experiment in creating optional boys' and girls' classes in the upper grades of his school. Mike was using Allen Jones's book, was rooted in the Bronx neighborhoods his students were growing up in, to get his boys excited about books and reading.

The physical appearance of the classroom blew Allen and me away. On the walls were three large posters that had Allen's book broken down year by year, with descriptions of important events taking place in the country and important events in Allen's life. To see the book broken down that way in a fourth-grade classroom was just incredible; neither of us, in our wildest dreams, ever imagined the book being used that way. Then while we looked at the display, the boys in the class came up to us, holding notebooks and pieces of paper, and asked us for our autographs. We took about five minutes signing the materials offered for every boy in the class, and then sat in chairs while Mike Napolitano had the boys sit on a carpet at our feet and ask us questions.

When the question period began it became clear that the boys knew Allen's story down to the minutest details, showing a particular fascination for his drug, prison, and basketball experiences. "Was your name in prison really Youngblood?" one boy asked. "Are there scars where you injected drugs?" another boy chimed in. "Did you hurt your hand when you dunked?" a third boy queried. "Who was the Whiz Kid (a famous Harlem drug dealer Allen referred to in one of his chapters)?" a fourth boy wanted to know. At least fifteen of the boys raised their hands and the discussion only ended, after more than thirty minutes, when Principal Cannon told us we had to leave. The enthusiasm of these boys about the contents of the book just overwhelmed us. Clearly, the stories Allen told touched a chord with these young people in a way no book they had been assigned in school had ever done. When Allen had to leave he called the boys together, asked them to put their hands in a circle, count to three, and chant, "I am somebody." They did exactly as Allen asked and SCREAMED the words out so loud the windows almost broke.

Allen and I left the classroom and the school feeling something truly extraordinary had taken place. A book we had written had validated the lives of teachers who were working in a South Bronx school, and had given one teacher a vehicle to create excitement about books and learning in a class of fourth-grade boys.

No television interview about the book or review in a major media outlet could match the feeling we had after spending a morning at PS 140. This is exactly why we had written this book!

WEDNESDAY, NOVEMBER 9, 2011

Letter to the Teachers of PS 140 in the South Bronx

To the Teachers of PS 140:

I want to thank you for your hospitality, your honesty, and your eloquent descriptions of the issues you face as educators during my presentation at your professional development day. It confirmed my conviction that the teaching staff of PS 140 provides a model of integrity, resilience, creativity, and commitment to students that those making education policy would do well to experience and observe firsthand.

No group in our society does a more difficult or important job than our public school teachers, and yet no group is more maligned and unjustly blamed for our society's problems. The result, as you all know, is that creative teaching, and the mentoring and relationship-building that accompanies all great teaching, is being undermined by excessive testing and the imposition of "accountability" standards based on student test scores that put teachers and school administrators under enormous stress.

But not everyone agrees that teachers should be the nation's punching bags! There is a growing number of people who feel that the work teachers are doing at schools like PS 140, which includes nurturing students, working with their families, and making the school a place where music, the arts, science, and history thrive, are what real education is all about. There is a reason why I take people from all over the world to visit PS 140 when I conduct tours of the Bronx. Right here, in this school, in the poorest congressional district in the nation, great things are taking place in every classroom and in a school community that embraces the culture and history of the neighborhood it is located in while trying to cope with the very real problems poverty creates for students and their families.

Someday, America will realize that this nation's true heroes are teachers in schools like PS 140, people who work under daunting conditions, in the face of great public skepticism and a misguided obsession with high-stakes testing, without ever losing their passion for their jobs or their love for the children they work with.

Please know that while I cannot change the direction of education policy in this city, this state, or the nation, I will stand up for you in every public forum I have access to, and point to PS 140 as an example of a public school that is a true community institution and a place that keeps the best traditions of American democracy alive in its day-to-day practice.

And also know that I will always be available to you to correspond, to talk, to visit your school and your classrooms and to help you fight for the respect you deserve and that you have earned.

With deepest appreciation,

Dr. Mark Naison
Professor of African American Studies and History
Fordham University
Founder and Principal Investigator
The Bronx African American History Project

SATURDAY, JULY 9, 2011

Why I Am Wary of Geoffrey Canada as a Social Commentator

I have been wary of Geoffrey Canada as a social commentator ever since he published a book called *Fist, Knife, Stick, Gun*, whose first section describes the Morrisania section of the South Bronx in the 1950s and 1960s as a hell-hole, a place plagued by violence and negativity. Violence and negativity there certainly was, but there were also great neighborhood sports programs, vibrant churches, great music and arts programs in the public schools, and many mentors and "old heads" who helped guide young people away from trouble. Canada's grim vision of this predominantly black section of the Bronx, contradicted by literally scores of interviews I did with people who lived in the same community, was a disturbing example of literary "tunnel vision"—an author's propensity to make his personal experience universal. By contrast, read Allen Jones's *The Rat That Got Away: A Bronx Memoir*, set in South Bronx housing projects and neighborhoods in the same time period, which recognizes that the same community could contain hustlers, political activists, striving students, gang leaders, protective parents, drug dealers, inspired teachers and mentors.

Today, Canada seems to apply the same tunnel vision to education when he views failing schools as the bane of struggling neighborhoods, and says that private business would never tolerate such failures. But such a comment could only be made by someone who doesn't examine the role of the private sector in America's inner city neighborhoods, which is to shut down operations and move out when neighborhood conditions and global economic trends make them unprofitable. While public schools in these communities remained open, factories have shut down, banks have closed their doors, insurance companies and banks have redlined the areas, landlords have abandoned and burned properties, and whole business districts have disappeared. In many cases, it was neighborhood public schools, hard-pressed and occasionally disorderly as they were (read Janet Mayer's wonderful book *As Bad as They Say: Three Decades of Teaching in the Bronx*), were the only places where young people could find support and inspiration when they were abandoned by private capital, and savaged by government cutbacks.

To now hold them as failures in an otherwise successful society can only be done by erasing what has happened in inner-city America in the last forty years. Global economic trends—coupled with government policies that siphoned wealth upward, and destabilized and instances destroyed inner-city neighborhoods—ruined these neighborhoods, not teachers unions and poorly run public schools.

MONDAY, JULY 11, 2011

A Bronx Tale: Questions for Those Who Argue That Failing Schools Cause Urban Decay

It has become fashionable for the right wing of the school reform movement, along with some progressives, to argue that failing schools are a major cause of the decay and stagnation in inner-city neighborhoods.

As a historian of the Bronx who has traced the borough's development from the 1930s to the present, I would like to raise a few questions about this formulation, based on important episodes in Bronx history.

First, when factory owners in the Bronx began closing their operations in the 1950s and 1960s, or moving them to other states or to countries, did they do so because the schools of the Bronx were failing, and the places they were moving their operations to (for example, South Carolina, Alabama, Haiti, the Dominican Republic), had better schools and a better-educated labor force? The resulting job losses devastated the Bronx's economy, but they were the result of factory owners' quest for cheaper labor, not for a better-educated labor force.

Second, when banks and insurance companies began redlining the Bronx, and landlords in the borough started burning their buildings to collect insurance money (a phenomenon that reached epidemic proportions from the late 60s through the late 70s), did they do so because the Bronx public schools were performing poorly, or did they do so because the job losses referred to in question one made it difficult for South Bronx tenants to pay their rent?

Third, when the city of New York, during the 1975 fiscal crisis, decided to eliminate music programs in the public schools, and shut down the after-school centers and night centers that had been fixtures in every public school in the city since the early 1950s, did they do so to punish the public schools for failing to educate their students properly, or because banks refused to lend money to keep the city government afloat unless drastic reductions were made to youth services no longer deemed "essential?"

Fourth, when a crack epidemic swept through the Bronx from the mid 1980s through the mid-1990's, did it do so because the schools were failing to do their job, or because young people in the Bronx gravitated to the underground economy, as there were no legal job opportunities available and youth recreation programs had been devastated by budget cuts?

Presented in chronological order, these were the four great tragedies that led the Bronx, once a place where upwardly mobile Black and Latino families moved to in search of better housing, better schools, and safer communities (from the 1930s through the 1950s) become a international symbol of urban decay and violence.

Can anyone seriously argue that "failing schools" were the major cause for this chain of disasters? Or were the causes to be found in global movements of capital; investment decisions by banks; landlords, and local businesses; and government policies that took resources and services out of Bronx neighborhoods and Bronx institutions, including public schools?

SATURDAY, JUNE 18, 2011
Fordham Alum/Bronx Teacher Denounces White House Education Policy

My Rant on Barack Obama's Facebook Page Today Saturday,
June 18, 2011 at 9:43pm
by Jenna Schlosbon

Shame on you, Barack Obama. I voted for you. I campaigned for you. I donated to you AND raised money for you. When I heard you speak about the problem of educational inequality in this country at the 2004 Democratic National Convention, I felt inspired. This is an issue that has been extraordinarily important to me for some time now, and I believed that you actually intended to do something about it. But instead, you continue to support the high-stakes testing agenda and businesslike competition among our public schools.

You and your secretary of education support tying teacher tenure/hiring/firing to standardized test scores. In so doing, you reduce children, particularly children of color who are living in poverty, to data points, forcing us to reduce our curriculum to incessant test prep for fear of a) having our schools shut down or b) losing our jobs. This is NOT education. This is a fear-based program. This puts a tremendous amount of stress on teachers and students alike. This is rote. This strips joy, curiosity, and creativity from learning. What about socio-emotional development? What about varied learning needs and learning styles? We need to educate the whole child, which these policies will not allow us to do. (And by the way, President Obama, Sidwell Friends, where you send your daughters, has stated that they do not believe tying teacher pay to student test scores is an effective measure of learning, evaluation, or progress.)

By upholding said policies you are just as bad as Klein, Bloomberg, and all of these other millionaire/billionaire pro-corporate "education reformers" who are "reforming" (destroying) our public schools in an effort to create something that benefits the corporate structure that controls this country: a mass proletariat who can unquestioningly obey, follow directions, and complete rote tasks INSTEAD of citizens who can question, or dare I say challenge, the status quo, formulate an opinion, think critically and creatively, or have any semblance of a moral compass.

We need freedom from high-stakes standardized tests and the freedom to make our curriculum more relevant to our students' lives, not only in an effort to engage them, but to show them how to be active citizens in their own communities, and perhaps even empower them to improve their communities.

President Obama, improving our public schools does not mean ridding schools of tenured, experienced educators and filling them with droves of twenty-year-olds (via TFA and other similar programs) as is the trend under current leadership in New York City. This only creates an atmosphere of chaos, confusion, stress, and eventual burnout and teacher turnover as these young teachers do not have the support of older veteran role models to show them the way. Although filling schools with young, untenured teachers, burning them out, and then cycling through the next batch may be smart financially (new teachers are the cheapest labor), high teacher turnover leads to further instability in our urban public schools that does very little to help impoverished students who, very often, already lack stability and structure at home.

Stop scapegoating and punishing teachers who do the best they can with the limited time and resources they have, and address the real reasons why our public school children, particularly urban public school children of color, are behind their wealthier white peers: poverty. Poverty affects students' nutrition and health, supervision and structure at home (which in turn affects attendance and homework completion/studying), living conditions . . . both inside and outside the home, parental education level, and these are only just a few examples. Our students' families need living wage jobs. Tax policy must be adjusted. No self-respecting, educated, hard-working professional can withstand being blamed day in and day out for the wounds of poverty that directly affect student learning and/or having his or her job threatened year after year due to "numbers" on these inane standardized tests.

Mr. Obama, you need to set the tone for real education reform, not the faux "reform" that these non-educator millionaires are propagating. End the teacher blaming. Let teachers teach. Stop supporting privatization, union-busting, and charter school takeovers, and start supporting our teachers and students by acknowledging that poverty impedes academic performance and actually discussing ways to address poverty in America. Tax policy and labor policy are two places to start.

Until you remove Arne Duncan as secretary of education and/or begin to acknowledge that the high-stakes testing business model is flawed and detrimental to our schools, I don't know that I can give you my vote in 2012, and educators across the country agree.

You will be hearing from me again and thousands upon thousands of educators, students, and other supporters at the Save Our Schools March on July 30th in Washington, DC.

When It Comes to Bronx Community History: Charter Schools Are Missing in Action

For the last ten years, I have had the privilege of leading one of the most exciting community history projects in the nation. The Bronx African American History Project, a collaboration between faculty in the Fordham Department of African and African American Studies and community-based scholars, has conducted more than three hundred oral history interviews, told the story of vibrant black neighborhoods in the Bronx never previously written about; uncovered a musical legacy of unmatched richness and variety; and most recently has begun charting the development of an African immigrant population that is the largest in the nation. Scholars from all over the country and all over the world have come to use our database, and our community tours have attracted groups from Germany, Denmark, Los Angeles, and Hartford, and groups from churches, universities, schools, and cultural organizations throughout New York City.

But perhaps the most gratifying portion of the research have been the opportunities we have been given to bring community history into the Bronx public schools. Seven years ago, a social studies coordinator in a Bronx school district, Phil Panaritis, invited me and a young colleague, Brian Purnell, to give presentations about BAAHP's research at a social studies conference for Bronx teachers; since then, responding to / accepting invitations to make presentations about the Bronx community has become routine in our work. I have given more than ten walking tours of historically black Bronx neighborhoods for school groups; done oral history training for teachers in thirteen Bronx schools; invited to speak at numerous school assemblies and graduation exercises; and have participated in at least five Teaching American History projects for Bronx teachers. One school in particular, PS 140 in Morrisania, has become an important community partner in our research, and has created an "old school museum" that honors the cultural traditions of the Morrisania neighborhood, and incorporated community history into all school celebrations. One of the school's signature events, a "schoolyard jam" highlighting jazz, doo-wop, salsa, and hip-hop—all music produced in South Bronx communities—was featured at the 2008 Convention of the Organization of American Historians as an example of an innovative history project in a public school, and written up in the *New York Times*.

In the course of organizing these events—which even included a Bronx-Berlin youth exchange involving an innovative Bronx high school, CUNY Prep—I have met scores of teachers, more than a few principals, and thousands of students, and the experience has left me convinced that community history can be an incredibly empowering aspect of school culture. But in thinking about this experience, I realized that one important school constituency was completely missing from our research project's community outreach—charter schools! Of the more than thirty elementary schools, middle schools, and high schools I have done community history programs for, not a single one was a charter school.

Given the number of charter schools in the Bronx, some of them run by national organizations like KIPP and Green Dot, and given the publicity our research has been given by the *New York Times*, the *Daily News*, and local cable outlets like Bronx Net and Cablevision, I do not think that omission is accidental. Charter school principals and teachers read newspapers and get invitations to participate in Teaching American History projects, but they seem to regard studying community history as a diversion rather than something that could better connect students to their neighborhoods and get them excited about learning history. The composition of their teaching staffs also contributes to this bias. Unlike Bronx public schools, which contain numerous veteran teachers who grew up in the neighborhoods where the schools are located, charter schools are filled with young teachers, many of them coming from alternative certification programs like Teach for America, who have no connections to the neighborhoods their schools are located. Furthermore, charter school teachers have been ordered to immerse their students in ritualized learning protocols designed to produce results on standardized tests.

This indifference to community history not only misses an opportunity to get students excited about acquiring historical knowledge, it also undermines an ideal of informed citizenship that encourages students to become active in improving their neighborhood. Both directly and indirectly, it suggests that everything valuable exists outside their communities, brought in by missionary teachers and administrators.

Make no mistake about it, if the Bronx is an example, charter schools are agents of depoliticization in communities that desperately need to know their histories and fight for their rights. Community history is a precious resource that administrators who know and love Bronx neighborhoods are excited to claim. Charter schools, in failing to claim this resource, reveal how little they are truly connected to the neighborhoods where they are located.

SATURDAY, JUNE 11, 2011

My Trip to a Rally Against School Budget Cuts at Lehman High School: Thoughts on Neighborhood, Teaching, and School Reform

On Friday, June 10, I left my office at Fordham around 2 p.m. to drive to a rally against education budget cuts at Herbert Lehman High School in the East Bronx, where I was slated to speak. I took the Bronx River Parkway South at Fordham Road, got off at East Tremont Avenue, and began a two-and-a-half-mile drive through the Bronx on East Tremont that took me through crowded, vital neighborhoods most residents of Manhattan and Upscale Brooklyn will never see.

On streets clogged with cars, trucks, city buses, gypsy cabs, and school buses, I observed a social and architectural landscape that resembled the Brooklyn of my youth, with different faces reflecting New York's current demographic profile. There wasn't a single luxury high rise in sight. The housing stock consisted of two- and three-family houses, brick, wood covered with aluminum siding. There are also apartment buildings ranging from four-story walkups, and to the twenty-plus eight- to ten-story buildings in the huge Parkchester development built in the 1940s that are now middle-income co-ops. The commercial strip was vibrant, filled with diners, furniture stores, used car lots and body shops, and rows of stores ranging from nail and hair salons to travel agencies, ethnic restaurants, and banks. There were several schools along the way, public and Catholic (including St. Raymond's High School), and schoolbuses everywhere. The sidewalks were as crowded as the streets, filled with schoolkids, mothers with young children, elderly people taking a stroll or going to the diner, and strong-looking men loading trucks and making deliveries. But what was most striking is that there were no visible signs of great poverty or great wealth. There were no vacant lots and storefronts, no food lines outside storefront churches, no idle young men hanging outside bodegas. There were also no health food stores, sushi bars, and hip young professionals sitting at tables outside cafes. What you had were crowds of working-class and middle-class New Yorkers of multiple ages, colors, and ethnicities, some black, some Latino, some South Asian, some white, going about their business purposefully on a hot Friday afternoon. To an old Brooklynite raised in a New York where the wealth was much more equally distributed than it is now, it felt familiar and it felt good.

After a forty-minute drive, I finally got to Lehman High School, a huge modernist building that sits atop the Hutchinson River Parkway, parked outside the diner across the street, and started looking for the rally. It was almost 3 p.m. and kids were pouring out of the school, thousands of them! This was by far the most diverse crowd I had seen at the more than ten Bronx high schools I had spoken at. There were many black and Latino students, but there were also a significant number of white and South Asian students as well. The students represented multiple cultural traditions. Women in hijabs, mostly South Asian, walked side by side with black, Latino, and white girls wearing tight shorts and low-cut tops; and the guys' outfits varied from football and baseball jerseys, to hip-hop and skater gear, to nicely ironed shirts and pants that could have come out of a JC Penney catalogue. For the most part, the kids looked happy, relaxed, and comfortable with one another. I didn't sense the fear or the air of menace that I sometimes felt outside Bronx high schools. I had to remind myself that this was a school that had been given an "F" by the New York City Department of Education (more on that later!), and had been assigned a team of School Turnaround Specialists to raise test scores and create a more positive atmosphere. From the outside at least, the school atmosphere looked just fine!

When I finally found the rally site, where a small group of teachers had assembled, along with a large number of police officers, I introduced myself and began preparing to participate in whatever capacity they wanted me to. The main organizers were two Latino men in their thirties or forties, and a white woman in her late twenties who had invited me to the rally, Anne Looser. Three or four teachers soon arrived to join us, all black or Latino women who appeared to be in their forties, along with a small group of students, and we began walking in a circle carrying signs that had been made for the occasion chanting "Bloomberg Says Cutback, We Say Fight Back!" The line of marchers kept growing rapidly. I was gratified to see that a former student of mine who lived in the neighborhood, Cathy Chan, had come to the rally with her boyfriend to show her support for the students and teachers at Lehman, but I was most pleased to see how many Lehman students joined the picket line. After fifteen minutes of marching, the group had grown to sixty-plus people, more than half of them students, and had created a loud and forceful protest visibly supported by many people in the area, including a group of firefighters who honked loudly in support as they drove by.

As the protest grew, a couple of things stood out for me. First was the incredible rapport between teachers and students that I saw on the picket line. The teachers assembled, whose number grew to over twenty by the time the protest ended, clearly knew students personally. From the comments exchanged and the hugs and high fives, they had relationships with them that extended beyond lecturer, tester, and grade giver. The rally chants that were unveiled when the students arrived in numbers also were telling in that they pinpointed what would be eliminated if the school lost funding:

Stop the Budget Cuts—No More Football!
Stop the Budget Cuts—No More Baseball!
Stop the Budget Cuts—No More Art Classes!
Stop the Budget Cuts—No More Theater!
Stop the Budget Cuts—No More Computer Classes!

Clearly, at this so-called failing school, students developed powerful relationships to teachers through activities like sports, the arts, and the cultivation of computer skills—activities that were are not seen by the current generation of school reformers as worthy of preservation in times of fiscal austerity.

And as I marched and chanted with these wonderful students and teachers who represented the heart and soul of immigrant working-class/middle-class New York, I thought if this is "failure" our city needs a lot more of them. The camaraderie and mutual appreciation I saw between teachers and students and students may not be quantifiable according to Race to the Top and No Child Left Behind, but it is more important than anything they are now measuring when it comes to determining the quality of public education. In a corner of the East Bronx, I saw a school of more than five thousand students that was an integral part of a vibrant, multi-cultural neighborhood, with teachers who loved their students, and who worked hard to bring out their talents inside and outside the classroom.

If what I saw and heard and experienced at Lehman High School can't be captured on existing tests and assessment systems, maybe it's time to throw out the assessments, not destroy what's positive in this remarkable school.

THURSDAY, MAY 5, 2011
Why More and More Students "In the Hood" Are Out of Control

During the last year, I have gotten more and more reports from the best teachers I know in Bronx public schools that their students "are out of con-trol." We are not talking about "Ivy League, Teach for America" types who grew up in wealthy suburbs, but tough, charismatic, physically imposing women, who are graduates of New York City public schools and have for-midable classroom management skills and great senses of humor.

At first, I found these reports hard to believe. The women I am talking about are not only physically strong, they are incredibly innovative in their pedagogy—the best of the best! If they can't control a class of Bronx eleven- or fourteen-year-olds, who could?

But then I started thinking about their work in a much larger context than one suggested by discussions of curriculum, class management, or graduation rates. And I came up with a startling conclusion—that students living in America's poor neighborhoods, even by age ten or eleven, already know, intuitively, that the schools they are in are unlikely to get them out of the world of poverty and hardship that surrounds them. As a result, they see what goes on in classrooms—especially all the tests they are bombarded with—as fundamentally irrelevant to their lives!

And they are not wrong in their assessment! If they look around their neighborhoods, they see precious few people who have used education to better their lives. For every person in their hood who gets out by pursuing higher education, there are five who leave by going to prison or joining the armed forces! In their world, there is little real-life reinforcement of the message schools preach—that the way to success in America is by passing tests, graduating from high school, and going on to college. Those who do manage to jump through all those hoops, find the path is long and treacherous in college—economically and academically—and if they do manage to get college degrees, they often can't get jobs at all. Or they can't get jobs that allow them to pay off their student loans.

The current economic crisis has only made the path of self-denial and academic effort seem more problematic. At a time when even middle-class college graduates from top private colleges have trouble finding work, how are you going to "sell" the proposition that education is the path to success in South Bronx neighborhoods like Morrisania or Hunts Point?

The bottom line is—in a city where the top one percent of the population monopolizes 44 percent of the income—you can't! The deck is already so stacked against youth growing up in poverty that no legerdemain, trickery, or classroom magic can convince them that the things they are learning and being tested on will have positive effects on their lives.

So why shouldn't they fool around? Why shouldn't they act out? Why shouldn't they try to enhance their reputation as a thug, a comedian, or a flirt by making the classroom their private theater? After all, those traits represent real-life social capital in the worlds they inhabit, as opposed to the math problems, history lessons, or sentences they are given to construct.

Some people attribute the phenomenon of poor kids acting out to the stress they are under outside of school, including poor diet, lack of sleep, gang violence, and physical abuse in their places of residence. These are are undoubtedly contributing factors. But let's not discount the "rational" element in student behavior, reflected in their very real understanding that the schools they are in are simply unable to deliver on the promise of a better life they use to "sell" their pedagogy.

Given that cold reality, there is absolutely no reason why a student in a place like the South Bronx should defer the joy and status of being a class comedian or "thug in training" for the prospect of participating in an endless round of test preparation, which for people in their neighborhood is truly "a race to nowhere."

FRIDAY, SEPTEMBER 21, 2012

The Bronx as an "Exercise Desert": New Language to Talk about the Health Crisis in Working-Class Communities

For the last few years, public health experts have used the term "food desert" to describe communities where residents lack access to healthy food, and suffer the twin problems of hunger and obesity. The Bronx has been identified as a classic example of such a food desert, and my students have written several term papers and theses demonstrating the difficulties of finding fresh fruits and vegetables in Bronx food stores, and of affording them even when they are available. One result is that the Bronx has the highest obesity rate of any borough in New York City, and one of the highest obesity rates of any county in the United States. But food is not the only health issue that the metaphor of a "desert" can be applied to. Bronx residents, especially young people, have so much difficulty finding opportunities for sports and recreation in the neighborhoods and their schools that the borough can be described as an "exercise desert" as well. The following are my criteria for describing a community as an exercise desert. I suspect many working-class communities around the nation would qualify:

1. Neighborhood schools do not offer regular gym classes during school days. Time once used for recess and gym are now devoted to test prep.
2. School gymnasiums, fields, and schoolyards, are not used on a daily basis for free or affordable sports and exercise programs (including dance), after school, either for their own students or community members.
3. There are few health clubs or community centers that offer regular sports and fitness programs that neighborhood residents, whether youth or adults, can afford.
4. Public parks are poorly maintained and have few, if any, youth sports leagues that use them on a regular basis.

If you live in a community where these conditions prevail, chances are that regular exercise will not be a part of your life and that the soccer leagues, baseball leagues, and dance classes that are a fixture of young people's lives in middle-class and wealthy neighborhoods, will reach only a tiny portion of neighborhood youth. The result—an epidemic of obesity and related health issues ranging from diabetes to circulatory problems—and another indication of how far race and class inequalities have deformed our national life.

SUNDAY, AUGUST 5, 2012

How "Race to the Top" Has Magnified the Obesity Problem in Poor and Working-Class Neighborhoods— a Bronx Perspective

When you walk through the gates of Fordham's Bronx campus onto Fordham Road, you are struck with an array of sounds and images that reflect the huge contrasts with the world you just left—the noise, the traffic, the bustling crowds, the energetic presence of children, almost all of them black and Latino. But another visual shock is the size of the people. On the Fordham campus, the vast majority of the students are slim and in shape, having bodies honed by hours in the gym as well as access to healthy food. On Fordham Road, most of the people, including the children, are heavy, some to the point of obesity. This contrast in body weight is, in some way, more striking than the racial differences. It is almost as if the people of the Bronx, overwhelmingly immigrant and working class, were a different species than those who go to school at Fordham. All throughout the Bronx, community activists and medical workers have been trying to address the borough's obesity problem, which has been intensified by poverty, lack of access to healthy food, and a dearth of affordable recreation opportunities. There are important experiments taking place in community-supported agriculture; attempts to convince local food stores to sell healthier produce; green carts and farmers markets; and widespread efforts to educate young people and families about the elements of healthy eating. Little by little, the Bronx's character as a "food desert" is being transformed, and there is some hope that within the next ten years its residents will have far more access to fresh fruits and vegetables, some of them grown in their own neighborhoods. Unfortunately, progress being made on the food front, is being undermined by backsliding on the recreation and exercise front thanks to education policies being promulgated in Washington and implemented by the state and city education departments. One of the requirements of the Race to the Top initiative is that states competing for funds must rate teachers based on student test scores and close schools, and remove their staffs, if test scores fail to reach a satisfactory level. New York State just received Race to the Top money and as a result, many schools in the city and state are now confronting the ordeal of annual testing in a condition of near panic.

Nowhere is this more true than in the Bronx, where test scores are the lowest in the city, and many schools have been already closed or designated for closing. This panic, felt as much by students and parents as by the teachers and principals fearful of losing their jobs, has resulted in a desperate effort to do everything possible to raise test scores. Not only have regular classroom sessions become monopolized by test prep, but many schools have turned recess and after-school recreation programs into study halls. Nowhere is such a consequence more damaging than in the Bronx. Young people already starved for recreation opportunities in their neighborhoods and spend huge amounts of time in front of a television set because their families are reluctant to let them play in the street, now find themselves without any significant time for exercise in school. If you think I am exaggerating, go visit Bronx schools or speak to people who work in them. Passing tests has become the overwhelming priority and pushed aside many other wonderful things schools can do, including promoting healthy lifestyles among their students.

What this means is that all the wonderful efforts being made to provide healthy eating options to Bronx residents will not have anywhere near the impact it should, because young people are being deprived of recreation opportunities in their schools during school hours and after school as well. Race to the Top is a very seductive title for an education initiative, but the young people of the Bronx, thanks to its policies, will be doing very little actual racing.

WEDNESDAY, JULY 18, 2012

Historian Vincent Harding Reflects on What Constitutes Great Teaching at an Urban Public High School

The following is an excerpt of an interview that we did for the Bronx African American History Project with historian and civil rights activist Dr. Vincent Harding at Morris High School in the South Bronx, Dr. Harding graduated as valedictorian in 1948. In it, he reflects on great teachers who influenced his life, and how his experience at Morris affected his future scholarship and activism. For example, Dr. Harding worked with Dr. King at the protests in Albany, Georgia, and Birmingham, Alabama; founded the Institute of the Black World; and advised the film series *Eyes on the Prize*.

Needless to say, his reflections have a certain relevance to current policy debates about what makes a great teacher.

Mark Naison: What I would like to do, if it's OK is turn to your high school experience. When we were talking before we went on tape, you said there were a number of memorable teachers you had at Morris. Could you tell us a little about your Morris experience?

Vincent Harding: That's a very important matter. When I first was applying to high school, I started out thinking that I was going to apply to the School of Aviation Technology, but someone wise told me that's probably not what you want to do, because that was more a technical school than anything else. And my next goal was Stuyvesant (a prestigious exam school). I had a tremendous amount invested in going to Stuyvesant because of the reputation of the school and because I was supposed to be a pretty bright person. And it was a marvelous experience for me to be to be to be rejected because even though I did well in math, I was not as good in math as some of the other applicants and so Stuyvesant was out. The next place I thought I should apply was Clinton, and it was only after Clinton said, "No, you are not in our area" that I considered Morris. It was kind of a last choice. And I was soon disappointed that I was being sent to Morris because I had heard that Morris was not nearly as good as these other places and it was a disappointment for a while. But as I said to you earlier, Mark, for me Morris played an absolutely crucial part in shaping my identity and my sense of purpose in the world.

When I came to the school for this interview, I was very happy to see the name Jacob Bernstein, the Morris principal when I was there, on the wall, because I remember him saying often that what he wanted to do was make Morris a real United Nations. He used that phrase often. And that whole idea of seeing diversity as something you're not forced into or trying to avoid, but something you welcome and try to shape into its best possibilities was a very important matter to me. Morris was an important counterpart for me to the church in Harlem I attended, Victory Tabernacle Church, and together they gave me the key elements of citizenship in a truly democratic society. Because what I had at Victory was a solid African American base from which I could move. I didn't stay there. I moved into the more diverse world that Morris represented. So that whole idea of moving from a particular cultural base into a larger society, into which you can bring something powerful out of that base, is something we Americans have to learn to do better. Now as for teachers, the most important teacher I had a Morris was a biology teacher. I never had her in a course, but she was my advisor, thank God. Her name was Ellen Bursler. I don't know how long she had been a biology teacher, but she provided something of tremendous importance, and that is that Mrs. Bursler loved me.

I was more than just a number on her list of advisees. She really came to the point where I knew she cared about me. And she got to know my mother, and my mother appreciated her, and she helped me find part-time and summer jobs because she knew that if I really wanted to go to college, I not only needed income, but exposure to a wider world—all that was part of her role as teacher. In my mind, I keep coming back to the image of her address in the upper-left-hand corner of the letters she constantly sent to me even when I was in college. "975 Knowlton Avenue" is what I would read. I would visit her house at times, meet her husband. She even invited me to her synagogue on a couple of occasions. She was for me the model teacher and she marked me for life through her deep concern and love for me.

The second person who comes to mind is a woman who taught French, Helen Prevost. And the impact she had on me was a little unusual. When I came to Morris, I had this side vision of myself as an athlete of some sort because in junior high school, I had been on the softball team. I always had enjoyed sports very much. But when I came to Morris, I acquired an interest in journalism and thought that I would like to write for the school paper, the *Morris Piper*. And it turned out that in this particular period, at the end of my first year at Morris, the tryouts for the *Piper* and the tryouts for the basketball team were on the same afternoon. And for reasons I don't fully understand, maybe knowing what she would say, I went to Mrs. Prevost, with whom I had been friendly, and asked "Mrs. Prevost, could you help me decide what I should do. Both of these tryouts are at the same time." And she said, "Basketball you can enjoy but for a very short time. Writing, journalism, you can do those your entire life." So I ended up going to the *Piper* and Mrs. Prevost was very important to me because going into journalism turned out to be a very important direction for me in my life.

MONDAY, JUNE 4, 2012

The Power of the Arts: A Bronx Tale

The following are excerpts from an oral history interview I did with trum-peter/composer/educator Jimmy Owens, who grew up in the Morrisania section of the Bronx and learned to play his instrument in the public schools of that borough. As public education is under attack throughout the nation, I want to take this opportunity to give a sense of the incredible arts instruction that once existed in the public schools of New York City. These programs allowed young people who made the band and orchestra in the junior high school to take home musical instruments to practice, and offered music instruction from teachers who themselves were often great musicians. As more and more arts instruction is being pushed out of our schools by test prep, and as public schools around the nation are starved of resources, I thought this little vignette might capture how some-thing precious is being lost if we continue to follow current policies to their logical conclusion.

Mark Naison: Who were your teachers at Junior High School 40 who had the biggest influence on you?

Jimmy Owens: I think the first teacher was the person who was in charge of the music department, Mr. Lightner. He was the person who came to PS 99 to give the students who were selected the special music aptitude test to see if we could go into a special class when we went to Jun-ior High School 40. I was lucky to pass the exam to be in that class. After Mr. Lightner, a new teacher came in the eighth grade. Her name was Edna Smith. I found out that she was a professional bass player who worked with a group called the Sweethearts of Rhythm. I played the trumpet. Ninth grade came the time for the exam for the High School of Music and Art and I said to her, "I want to take the exam for Music and Art," so she started to ask me questions and I didn't know them well. She then said, "You can't just play good and get in. You have to know music theory." So she started to teach me the scales, and she started to teach me the key signatures. I re-member she taught me key signatures up to four flats and four sharps.

MN: So you had not been reading music before?

JO: Well I was reading music, but I was kind of cold reading my music. It wasn't something that was emphasized. So she—Ms. Smith—taught me this stuff. I had three or four weeks before the exam and I would go to her room after school for individual instruction. Then on Saturday, sometimes I would go and meet her at her house. She lived over on Fulton Avenue near Bronx Hospital. Sometimes, she would meet me at the beauty parlor rather than her house because she was always there getting her hair done. While she was in the chair, she would say, "What's the key with one flat? What is that flat? Explain the scale to me."

MN: What did the other people [around] think?

JO: I never thought about them, but she was nice and would introduce me to all the people by saying "He's going to be a great young musician." I wound up getting into High School of Music and Art thanks to Ms. Smith and stayed in touch with her for the first year, periodically going back to JHS 40 to see her. Then she left one or two years after and went to teach somewhere else. I lost track of her.

MN: When you were graduating from Junior High School 40, were you playing in any venues in the community?

JO: Yes.

MN: Where were some of the places you would be performing at that time?

JO: The only places that I could perform was at the community centers and auditoriums. There was a group of us who were learning how to play and we would use these places for jam sessions.

MN: Who were some of the people in these jam sessions?

JO: We would go into Harlem and there would be a trumpet player named Faruk Daud, who wrote the song "Daud" for his father Talib Daud. He played with Dizzy Gillespie. Pianist Larry Willis and alto saxophonist Johnny Simon were from the Bronx. At PS 99, we used the auditorium because there was a guy by the name of Mr. Tibbs. He was a real community person who took us all under his wing. Mr. Tibbs was a physical education teacher. He would present a concert and have alto saxophonists Lou Donaldson and Jackie McLean come by and play in the auditorium.

SATURDAY, APRIL 28, 2012

Why High School Students Will Ultimately Take the Lead in Protests Against Corporate School Reform—View from the Bronx

This spring, one of my best students just completed a brilliant senior thesis on what the school experience is like for students who attend the six high schools, in what was once Roosevelt High School, across the street from Fordham's Bronx campus. The picture is not a pretty one. Students have to pass through metal detectors to enter schools with "zero tolerance" policies for infractions ranging from wearing a hat, to being found on a different floor than the one your school is located on, or going to the bathroom without permission. Some of these infractions lead to suspensions; if you protest too vigorously, they could lead to arrest.

The classroom experience is little better. Students describe classes almost strictly confined to memorizing material for New York State Regents exams. When students begin discussing interesting subjects, teachers shut the discussion down for fear it might undermine student performance upon tests, which their own careers now rely on. Though teachers try to help students and clearly care for them, they are visibly under extreme stress because of fear that if test scores don't improve, their schools might be closed and they will lose their jobs. The fear spills over into the treatment of students who repeatedly fail tests, or who have multiple behavioral infractions. Such students are subtly, and not so subtly, encouraged by school administrators to drop out of school lest they undermine the school's test profile, or the atmosphere of disciplined obedience required for relentless test prep.

Students at the schools in question are resentful, but not explicitly politicized. They rebel, but the ways they rebel take the form of what historian Robin Kelley called "the hidden transcript," rather than strikes and walkouts. Students who have been disciplined for violating school rules, or are just resentful about the police state atmosphere, have all kind of ways of showing their contempt. They go out of their way to argue with or "bait" police and security officers; they come late and leave early; they start fights with fellow students, or insult and challenge teachers. But at some point, as the communities they live in become more politicized, which is starting to happen in the Bronx, especially around the issues of police violence and racial profiling, these students are going to ask some hard questions about what they are being put through in the name of getting an education. And what they conclude may be something like this: "Wait a minute, we are being asked to spent six hours a day doing nothing but sitting at our desks memorizing material for tests, so we can graduate from high school and do what? Go to a college we can't afford? Get a job working in a fast-food restaurant or a big-box realtor? Join the military? And even if by some chance we do go to college, is the result worth it when we finally graduate? What do we get? Tens of thousands of dollars of student loan debt and jobs that don't offer salaries sufficient to pay them off?"

The young people my student interviewed are nowhere near that point yet, but they are starting to realize that something is very wrong. It is one thing to subject yourself to prisonlike conditions and militarized discipline if the result is escape from poverty, and a ticket to the good life. But what if neither of those results from all this sacrifice? When that realization begins to sink in, and as students see protests in their neighborhoods against stop-and-frisk, racial profiling, evictions and foreclosures, and closings of day care centers and after-school programs, don't be surprised of these students follow the example of neighborhood activists. They may begin organizing strikes and walkouts to demand that schools be places where real learning takes place, and where there are extracurricular activities that make school interesting and nurture skills students value.

There are signs of these kind of high school protests happening around the country—in Detroit, in Maryland, in some portions of New York City. But they are going to expand incrementally in the next few years, as justice activism spreads into working-class neighborhoods, and as corporate education reform erodes even more student rights. In elementary schools, parents will be the ones taking the lead against corporate school reform; in high schools it will be the students. From my point of view, anything we can do to promote this day of reckoning is positive. Organizing Freedom Schools in inner-city and working-class neighborhoods that allow students to critically assess their surroundings would be one big step in that direction.

WEDNESDAY, JANUARY 30, 2013
A Bronx Story with Relevance to the Murders in Chicago

It's the mid-1950s. Howie Evans, a fifteen-year-old, up-and-coming basketball and track star, is shooting hoops in the night center at PS 99 in the Morrisania section of the Bronx, which like most elementary school gymnasiums in New York City, was kept open five nights a week from 3 to 5 p.m. and 7 to 9 p.m. with supervised activity. All of a sudden, two of Howie's friends rush into the gym. Their mostly Puerto Rican gang, of which Howie is a member, is having a rumble with a much-feared black gang called the "Slicksters." The head of the night center, Vincent Tibbs, a powerfully built African American teacher who was a friend to many young people in the neighborhood, overheard what was going on and walked slowly over to the door of the gym. When Howie tried to rush out, Mr. Tibbs stood in front of the door and said, "I'm not letting you leave here. You have a future. You're not going to die in the street." Howie, who told me this story during an oral history interview I did with him, screamed and cried. But Mr. Tibbs, who had the strength and appearance of a weightlifter, wouldn't move. Howie ended up missing the rumble. It is well he did, because two young men died that night, and this was more rare in a time before guns were common weapons on the streets of New York. And Mr. Tibbs was right. Howie did have a great future. He went on to become a teacher, a youth center director, a college basketball coach (which is how I met him), and the sports writer for the *Amsterdam News*, a position he holds to this day.

But the story is not just about Howie, it's about the incredible after-school and night centers that were fixtures in every single public school in

New York City until they were closed down during New York City's fiscal crisis of the 1970s. These centers (I attended one religiously in Brooklyn) had basketball and nok hockey, arts and crafts, and music programs and held tournaments and dances. Some of them, like the PS 99 Center, held talent shows that spawned some of New York City's great doo-wop and Latin music acts. But all of them had teachers like Mr. Tibbs who provided supervision, skill instruction, mentoring, and sometimes life-saving advice to two generations of young men and women who attended the city's public schools, a good many of whom lived in tough working-class neighborhoods like Morrisania.

Now let's segue to Chicago, where young people are killing one another at an alarming rate. The schools in that city are in upheaval; many have been closed, some are faced with closing, teachers and students are being told that their school's fates depend on how well students score on standardized tests; some of which have been installed at the expense of arts, music, and sports programs in the schools. Those in charge of education, locally and nationally, think these strategies will improve educational achievement. But what happens in these schools after regular school hours finish? Do they offer safe zones for young people in Chicago's working-class and poor neighborhoods? Do they have arts and sports programs that will attract young people from the streets? Do they have teachers/mentors like Mr. Tibbs who will take a personal interest in tough young men and women, and place their own bodies between them and the prospect of death through gang violence? If the answer is no—that these schools are largely empty once classes end and do little or nothing to attract young people—maybe it's time to start rethinking current school programs. Wouldn't it be better to have a moratorium on all policies—like school closings, which destabilize neighborhoods, and invest in turning schools into round-the-clock community centers the like in New York City, when Howie Evans was growing up? And if the problem is money, how about taking the money currently spent on testing and assessment and use it to create after-school programs where caring adults offer activities that build on young people's talents and creativity?

But to do this, we have to rethink the roles school play in neighborhoods like the Bronx's Morrisania and Chicago's Humboldt Park, and not view them as places to train and discipline a future labor force, but places that strengthen communities, and nurture young people into become community-minded citizens. To do that, we have to also treat teachers differently, and respect those who have made teaching a lifetime profession, and are committed to nurturing and mentoring young people, even in the most challenging circumstances.

If we don't do that kind of reconfiguration of our thinking and our policies, we are likely to mourn a lot more young people killed by their peers, and not just in Chicago.

FRIDAY, FEBRUARY 8, 2013

Donald Byrd and the Power of Music Instruction Inside and Outside Our Public Schools

I just found out that the great jazz trumpeter, composer, and music innovator Donald Byrd passed away. I am devastated by this news, not only because Donald Byrd owned a brownstone on the Park Slope block where I moved in 1976, but because Donald Byrd was a central figure in the musical history of the Bronx, which I discovered when doing oral histories for the Bronx African American History Project. In the 1950s, Donald Byrd and Herbie Hancock got an apartment together on Boston Road and 164th Street in the Bronx in Morrisania, then the Bronx's largest and most vital black neighborhood. Byrd was working as a music teacher at Burger Junior High School near St. Mary's Park, a common destination for great musicians when New York City middle schools and high schools had bands, orchestras, and hundreds of instruments that students with talent could take home to practice. During his years in the Bronx, Byrd mentored many talented younger musicians, among them jazz trumpeter Jimmy Owens, who took private lessons from Byrd; and salsero and trombone player Willie Colón, who was his student at Burger JHS. But the most amazing Byrd story has to do with his role in the recording of Mongo Santamaria's "Watermelon

Man." One day, in the early 1960s, Mongo Santamaria called up Herbie Hancock and asked him to sit in as a pianist with Mongo's band, which was then performing at Club Cubano Inter Americano on Prospect Avenue, a popular Latin music spot. Herbie was reluctant to do it because he never played Latin before, but accepted the offer and was doing pretty well by the end of the first set. Then during intermission, Donald Byrd, who was there, asked Herbie to play his original composition "Watermelon Man" for Mongo. When Herbie started doing this, Mongo's band, especially his huge percussion section, started joining in, and before you knew it the whole club was dancing. Mongo was so excited by what happened that he asked if he could record the song. He did, and it became his greatest hit. Such is the influence that Donald Byrd had as a teacher and a mentor to young musicians. It is not only a testimony to his own unique vision, and to black-Latino cultural and musical cross-fertilization, it is a reminder of how important it is to keep music instruction and music performance as an integral part of the life of our public schools.

Afterword

The Rise of the Badass Teachers Association: A Brief History

The Badass Teachers Association began as a modest attempt to capitalize on the energies of a parent-led test revolt that took place in New York during the spring of 2013 and turned, unexpectedly, into a huge protest movement by teachers across the nation.

In April 2013, about ten thousand families decided to opt their children out of state tests in New York. One of the strongest centers of this movement was on Long Island, where conservative and libertarian parents joined with liberal and progressive parents to protest the huge amount of testing in local schools. They thought these practices were making good schools worse, and creating near-abusive levels of stress for children and families.

As an education activist whose university affiliation appeared to give legitimacy to the protest, I was invited to speak at several rallies sponsored by one of the groups formed in the course of the New York test revolt—Parents and Teachers Against the Common Core (PTACC)—and was blown away by how those holding differing views on non-education issues were able to work together, and even begin liking one another. I made friends with some of the organizers of PTACC, and together we formed a Facebook group called the Badass Parents Association to capitalize on this energy, and this new "multipartisan approach." In a month, we attracted about three hundred members, and were really proud of ourselves for drawing in that number of people!

Then, in mid-June, one of the people I met through the Badass Parents group, an education activist from Oklahoma named Priscilla Sanstead, suggested we form a Badass Teachers Association Facebook page to help recruit teachers to support parents and students protesting high-stakes testing. What happened next absolutely stunned us! We formed the group at 4:30 p.m. on Friday, June 14, and by Saturday night, we had three hundred members, as much as the Badass Parents Association had acquired in a month; and these teachers were from all over the country.

In response to this unexpected influx, one of the first people who joined the group—a brilliant teacher and parent-activist named Marla Massey Kilfoyle, a leader of the Long Island test revolt—suggested we organize a recruiting contest, and declare the winner "Badass Teacher of the Month." I set up the contest for between 4 and 5 p.m. on Sunday, June 16 and the results were even more astonishing. More than a thousand people were recruited into the group in that one hour! Clearly, the name—which implies that teachers throughout the nation are *fed up* with how they are being treated by the press, the public, and leaders of both parties—was touching a huge chord with teachers everywhere.

Over the next week, the group started adding nearly a thousand people a day and the three of us at the center of this movement—me, Priscilla, and Marla—tried to make sense of what was happening and steer it in a constructive direction. Why was this outpouring of rage and defiance coming now? The first reason was that all over the country, teachers were under attack—their lessons were being scripted; their careers were being threatened by test-based evaluation systems; and they were forced to teach in ways that undermined their autonomy and professional integrity. But most importantly, the large portion of the nation's teachers who had considered themselves Democrats or liberals had become totally disillusioned with the Obama administration's education policies, which were as much or more responsible for making their daily lives miserable the Bush administration. They felt totally isolated and alone—without *any* friends in high places—and they were ready to fight back.

Our job, we quickly concluded, was to give them an organizational structure capable of doing that. Fortunately, my two cofounders are organizational geniuses, and many of the teachers who joined the group were computer-savvy, artistically talented, and expert at using social media. While I wrote public pronouncements to explain why the group had grown so fast, my colleagues created a board of administrators to run the organization and set policy, and developed a network of state BAT organizations capable of holding meetings and launching protests on the ground. And we encouraged all our members to use multimedia techniques—especially memes and music videos—to get the group's message across creatively.

Within a month, we had recruited close to twenty thousand members and were starting organize actions and warn those most responsible for anti-teacher policies and statements—Michelle Rhee, Secretary of Education Arne Duncan, Bill Gates, and others—that there was a new militant teacher group that was coming after them. We were so effective—through social media, as well as traditional means of protest—that we were publicly endorsed by the nation's most important education historian and critic, Diane Ravitch.

Fast forward to the present. We are now a little more than six months old and show no signs of falling apart. We have more than thirty-six thousand members, launch actions every week, and are planning a Teachers March on Washington on July 28, 2014, with plans for fifty thousand angry teachers to surround the US Department of Education.

There is nothing accidental about our growth. America's teachers are tired of being the favorite punching bags of leaders of both political parties and are—through this group—saying, "enough is enough."

Acknowledgments

This book is a collective product, the result of experiences, discussions, and debates with many amazing people. First of all, I want to thank all the teachers, principals, and school support staff in the Bronx who welcomed me when I came into their schools to do community history projects and who, when given the opportunity, transformed the research I had done into living, breathing examples of community enlightenment and empowerment. It is the unfair attacks on these individuals and the institutions they have devoted their lives to that led me to undertake the work of teacher advocacy and education activism that is the subject of this book.

Second, I want to thank the activists I met in the Save Our Schools movement and in United Opt Out once I began speaking out on education issues. There are scores of people I could thank, but I want to give a special shout-out to Dave Greene and Peggy Robertson, the two people most responsible for my coming to Washington, DC, to talk about what I had seen and experienced in Bronx schools, and who connected me to their own incredible networks of activism, which now have become permanent parts of my life.

Third, I want to thank my long-term friend, comrade, and fellow activist, Dr. Henry Taylor of SUNY Buffalo, who has been a continuous source of inspiration because of his own innovative work in community development, and who has always insisted that our research has to be translated into projects that transform the lives of marginalized and forgotten people. His example, as well as his sage advice, has shaped many of the essays in this book.

Fourth, I want to thank two outstanding educators, Priscilla Sanstead and Marla Kilfoyle, who sensed the growing rage and alienation among America's public school teachers and helped me found that improbable organization, the Badass Teachers Association, which has changed the face of education activism in the United States.

And finally, I want to thank my wife Liz Phillips, the most brilliant educator I know; a neighborhood legend whose wisdom, passion, and example of selfless service to her school community reminds me of what is possible in public education when great teaching and leadership is unleashed. I have learned so much about education policy from conversations with Liz, but I've learned even more from watching how hard she works and seeing how much she cares about the teachers, students, parents, and school personnel she interacts with daily. The people I have mentioned represent the heart and soul of public education in the United States. It is because of them I have found a voice. It is because of them that I fight.

Index

About the Author

Mark Naison is professor of African American studies and history at Fordham University. He is the author of many books and articles including *Communists in Harlem During the Depression* and *White Boy: A Memoir*. The founder of the Bronx African American History project, Naison has emerged in the last five years as a passionate defender of America's public school teachers and students, founding groups like Dump Duncan, the Teachers Talk Back Project, and most recently, the Badass Teachers Association.